The Chef's Table

The Chef's Table

Restaurant-Inspired Recipes for the Home Chef

Lucy Waverman   James Chatto   Tony Aspler

RANDOM HOUSE CANADA

First published in Canada by Random House Canada, a division of Random House of Canada Limited.

Random House Canada and colophon are trademarks.

Canadian Cataloguing in Data Publication

Waverman, Lucy
    The chef's table

Includes index.
ISBN 0-679-31039-8

1. Cookery – Ontario – Toronto. I. Chatto, James II. Aspler, Tony 1939- .
III. Toronto Taste (Association). IV. Title

TX715.6.W378 2000   641.5'09713'541   C00-930212-3

Cover and interior design: Sharon Foster Design
Cover photograph and interior colour photography: Vince Noguchi
Interior black and white photography: Per Kristiansen
Author photograph: Lorreanne Jones

Printed and bound in Canada

Front cover: Chilean Black Sea Bass with Mustard Crust and Ginger Soy Mirin Sauce (page 105)

10 9 8 7 6 5 4 3 2 1

MESSAGE FROM THE BOARD OF DIRECTORS

Over the past decade, executive chefs from Toronto's finest restaurants have devoted one day in June to prepare and serve samplings of their incredible gourmet creations at a special fundraising event. Called Toronto Taste, this annual fundraiser is organized by Second Harvest, Toronto's not-for-profit perishable food rescue program. Now in its tenth year, the event has raised almost two million dollars to help feed thousands of hungry and homeless people in the city.

On that summer day in June, guests stroll from tent to tent sampling amazing dishes created on-site by more than sixty chefs while sipping the finest complementary wines. This book recreates the experiences of dining at the chef's table of your choice by enabling you to prepare these fabulous dishes in your own kitchen.

We would like to thank Canadian experts in food, dining and wine—Lucy Waverman, James Chatto and Tony Aspler—for pooling their formidable talents to produce *The Chef's Table*. This unique recipe collection, featuring some of the best dishes served at Toronto Taste through the years, includes the wine recommendations of a connoissseur and engaging profiles of the chefs and their restaurants. The recipes are peppered with secrets from the kitchens of our most notable restaurants and tested by experts, so you can rely on the results.

On behalf of Second Harvest, we would like to thank the fine restaurants and talented chefs who support Toronto Taste. We are also grateful to the publisher, Random House Canada, for donating the profits of *The Chef's Table* to our cause. And we extend our appreciation to the volunteers who have helped make Toronto Taste an enormous success year after year.

Second Harvest also acknowledges the many supermarkets, restaurants, caterers and food companies that donate raw and prepared foods to our cause. In addition, we would like to thank our individual and corporate cash donors as well as the countless volunteers who have contributed to our efforts since the founding of Second Harvest in 1985.

Toronto Taste is pivotal in helping to raise the funds Second Harvest needs to rescue fresh, perishable food. For each dollar raised, we can collect and deliver enough food for three meals. This efficiency is something for which we are justifiably proud.

Thank you for all your support and bon appetit!

The Board of Directors of Second Harvest
Toronto, Ontario

Contents

SECOND HARVEST
A Fresh Approach To Hunger

Second Harvest: A History of Food Rescue

Since its beginning fourteen years ago, Second Harvest has been fulfilling a simple mandate: to rescue surplus, perishable food and deliver it to agencies in Toronto that provide meals to people in need. Despite tremendous growth in the size of the organization, its goals remain unchanged: to raise awareness of the problem of hunger in Toronto and, each year, to distribute increased quantities of food.

In 1985, Ina Andre and Joan Clayton recognized the need for a perishable food rescue program. The two friends, who had been active in efforts to alleviate hunger in developing countries, began collecting and delivering surplus food in Toronto from the back of a station wagon. Second Harvest was born.

In 1999, Second Harvest distributed over three and a half million pounds of food in refrigerated trucks and provided the makings for an estimated three million meals.

Sadly, the organization's growth has been driven by an escalating need. An estimated 38 percent of Toronto's children under the age of 10 live in poverty—an increase of 66 percent since 1991. Families and youth are now the fastest growing groups to experience homelessness. Currently over 1,000 children live in shelters for the homeless.*

The good news is that Second Harvest helps by providing donated fresh food daily to 110 social agencies in Toronto. To accomplish this, it has established a stable, consistent supply of high-quality, fresh food. Grocery stores, for example, provide a daily source of produce, meat, bakery and deli products for immediate distribution and use. As a result, recipient agencies can provide a more varied and nutritionally balanced diet to their clients. Second Harvest also allows agencies to plan on the basis of a consistent supply of food, and that enables the allocation of precious dollars to other areas such as programming that addresses root causes of problems or enhances life skills.

Second Harvest's success in fundraising allows it to continue its essential work. For the past ten years, Toronto Taste has raised approximately one-third of the annual operating budget. We are proud to celebrate its tenth anniversary. Over the decade, Toronto Taste has inspired hundreds of chefs, vintners, brewers and dedicated volunteers to participate in the event that draws over 1,000 patrons each year.

On behalf of the people in Toronto whom we serve, Second Harvest thanks you for sharing in this celebration.

* Source: Action Plan for The Children's Report Card 1999

ACKNOWLEDGMENTS

Second Harvest is proud to acknowledge the sponsors of the 10th Anniversary Toronto Taste.

The Daniels Corporation will celebrate its fifth year of support as Presenting Sponsor of the 10th Anniversary event. In sponsoring Toronto Taste, Daniels continues its vital support of organizations providing food, clothing and shelter. **Pusateri's Fine Foods & Catering** has donated its surplus perishable food to Second Harvest for over a decade. The 10th Anniversary event marks Pusateri's third year as Headline Sponsor. **Evian Natural Spring Water,** a third-year Sommelier Sponsor, also generously supplies its refreshing beverage for guests and chefs each year. **The Housesitters** joined as a Sommelier Sponsor in 1999. The company also contributes its housesitting services to the event's silent auction and raffle prizes. **Renée's Gourmet** has been a Maitre d' Sponsor for numerous years. Its sauces and salad dressing are a staple on the shelves of the Toronto Taste Market. **Weber-Stephen Products Co.,** joined as a Maitre d' Sponsor in 1999. The barbecues Weber donates to the silent auction cause bidding wars each year! **Lever Pond's,** a Maitre d' Sponsor since 1997, supports Second Harvest throughout the year at various events. **Lombard Insurance Companies,** another loyal corporate supporter annually, returns for its second year as Maitre d' Sponsor. Labatt's Breweries introduces **Stella Artois,** an upscale European beer, as a Maitre d' Sponsor in 2000. Entrée Sponsors, **MDS Inc., Kingsmill Foods Co., Ltd.** and **Zev Daniels Architects** have all renewed their support by adding their sponsorship to the 10th Anniversary event. Our media sponsors, **Toronto Life, CFRB.AM.1010, toronto.com** and **President's Choice Magazine** have become Toronto Taste's annual ambassadors, communicating the news of the event to the public. **Enbridge Consumers Gas,** a supporter since year one, provides barbecues en masse each year for the chefs cooking al fresco. **United Airlines,** a sponsor since 1998, provides travel prizes that make the Toronto Taste raffle the envy of charitable events in Toronto.

Of course, Toronto Taste would not be complete without the vast array of beverages presented each year. Many of this year's sponsors have made Toronto Taste a must-attend annual event. Salut! Atlas Wines Inc., Big Rock Brewery Ltd., Brick Brewing Co. Limited, Brunello Wine Imports, California Wine Imports, Cave Spring Cellars, Château des Charmes, Colio Estate Wines, Creemore Springs Brewery Ltd., DuChasse Wines & Spirits, Henry of Pelham Estate Winery, Inniskillin Wines Inc., J. Cipelli Wines & Spirits, Kittling Ridge Ltd., Lifford Agencies Limited, Maxxium Canada, Nihco International Ltd., Oland Specialty Beer Co., Philippe Dandurand Wines, Pillitteri Estates Winery Inc., Prevedello Imports, Russell Woodman Agency, Seagram Canada, Sleeman Brewing & Malting Co. Ltd, Southbrook Farms Winery, Strewn Winery & The Wine Country Cooking School, Upper Canada Brewing Company, Vineland Estates Winery, Vinvino Wine Merchants

Quite simply, Toronto Taste could not enjoy its remarkable success without the support of its loyal sponsors. Second Harvest extends appreciation to them all.

AUTHOR ACKNOWLEDGMENTS

This book is the collaboration of many people who gave their time and talent on a volunteer basis to help the cause of Second Harvest. Photographs always add to a cookbook. For this book, Vince Noguchi took the dazzling color photography, Jennifer McLagan was responsible for the sophisticated food-styling and prop stylist Shelley Tauber made the pictures come to life. The stellar black and white photography was taken by Per Kristiansen. Many thanks to Pusateri's for contributing the food for the mouthwatering photographs.

A cookbook is only as good as its recipe testers and we were fortunate to have so many dedicated individuals. Lesleigh Landry headed the committee and did great work in coordinating the testing. They all put a huge effort into ensuring the recipes were perfect.

Heartfelt thanks to the many people who generously contributed their time for this project:

Recipe Testers:
Donna Bartolini, Laura Buckley, Vicki Burns, Sasha Chapman, Riki Dixon, Carolyn Gall Casey, Sarah Hobiak, Heather Howe, Lesleigh Landry, Joanne Leese, Jennifer Mackenzie, Jan Main, Kim Masin, Daphna Rabinovitch, Emily Richards, Ettie Shuken, Therese Taylor, Susan Van Hezewijk, Adell Schneer, Tracy Syvret, Susan Thompson, Nicole Young

Photographers:
Vince Noguchi, Ray Fong, Per Kristiansen

Food Stylist:
Jennifer McLagan

Prop Stylist:
Shelley Tauber

Food:
Pusateri's Fine Food and Catering

Beer:
Stephen Beaumont

INTRODUCTION

This cookbook happened because many people believed in it.

Jacqueline Inwood, event coordinator for Toronto Taste, began it all by approaching David Kent at Random House for a contribution to Toronto Taste. He took this request to his staff and came back with the idea for a book that would be a fundraising venture and a wonderful cookbook in its own right.

Random House Canada, who will be donating the proceeds of sales of *The Chef's Table* to Second Harvest, pulled together a team under the auspices of Sarah Davies. Sarah found the finest people in their fields to create the best book we could. Shelley Tanaka had the daunting task of editing a diverse collection of recipes—she succeeded brilliantly as always. The elegant yet friendly design is a Sharon Foster original.

As a board member of Second Harvest and a cookbook author, I volunteered to select the recipes, write about the food and insert tips, techniques and explanations where necessary. I enlisted help from the eloquent James Chatto, who brings alive the personalities of the chefs on the printed page, and leading wine writer Tony Aspler, who matched the food with both Canadian and international wines. We are all proud of this stylish and accessible book.

The greatest challenge presented by this book was to maintain the integrity of the chefs' recipes while also making them work for the home cook. With nine years worth to choose from, we tried to pick recipes that were popular at Taste and showcased the chefs and their restaurants. Some chefs have moved on, and some restaurants are no more, but if they were an integral part of the food scene you will find some culinary memories here.

Home cooks are suspicious of chef-oriented cookbooks because of their often elaborate and sophisticated nature. *The Chef's Table* is different. Most of the ingredients used in this book are available throughout the country, but if not, substitutions are suggested. Some techniques may be a little unusual, but again, alternate methods are offered.

Although most of the chefs in this book reside in Ontario, we have expanded their culinary vision so that the dishes can be produced in home kitchens from Vancouver to Halifax. Many of the recipes were initially developed to produce finger food for more than one thousand people who have supported Toronto Taste annually. As we tested the recipes, we got a feel instantly for how each chef's food ideas could play a role in your own dinner party. These dishes define what it means to entertain.

Adding pleasure to your enjoyment of these exciting recipes are James Chatto's superbly written and humorous essays—this man loves to eat! Tony Aspler's insight into and knowledge of the Canadian wine scene helps complete the creation of the restaurant experience in your own home. And as an additional bonus, for those times when only beer will do, Stephen Beaumont offers some excellent choices.

It was a delight to work on the book and an honour to have been part of creating it for such an important cause.

Lucy Waverman

Ask any chef or caterer, cook or restauranteur why they are happy to give up a precious Sunday to take part in Toronto Taste, and you'll hear the same three answers: because they believe in the vital importance of the work done by Second Harvest; because Taste really is a gourmet gala, surely the most successful, flamboyant and relevant of all the many charitable events to which they contribute; and also because it's such a terrific day out. This is a chance for men and women who work long, antisocial hours in noisy, windowless kitchens to remember that they are part of a broader profession. They stroll from table to table, greeting old friends, introducing their assistants, swapping gossip and jokes, discreetly checking what everyone else has decided to serve. There is excitement in the air, a holiday atmosphere, like a celebratory party or some long-awaited reunion. Then the first ticket holders appear and white jackets are hurriedly buttoned, stoves lit, table decorations given a final tweak. As crowds start to gather, the energy levels soar. For once, those who cook and those who eat are face to face, without the kitchen door, the corps of waiters, and all the distancing rituals of a restaurant between them. "Taste this! Do you like it?" Moans of pleasure: "Oh wow! That is *so* delectable!" Direct communication, instant gratification on both sides of the table, a delicious moment shared. In the end, that's what it's all about. Toronto Taste, Second Harvest itself and this book of recipes are variations upon a single, profoundly simple theme: the importance of sharing.

James Chatto

WINE AND FOOD MATCHING

In matching wines with the recipes in this book I have chosen both Canadian and imported products. The selections are generic styles of wine that will complement the dishes. This does not mean that the adventurous host must stick to a specific wine I have matched with the food. The suggestions are merely a guide to the type of wine that will enhance the pleasure of the dining experience.

There are many people who never think about matching food and wine because their first and most urgent need is to ensure that their families don't go hungry. In purchasing a copy of *The Chef's Table* you make a valuable contribution to Second Harvest, a charity whose aim is to ensure that those of us who have the luxury of choosing our menu can help support those who cannot.

Tony Aspler

Hors d'oeuvre

ACE BAKERY

[ANDREA STEWART]

One of the great retail success stories of the 1990s, Ace Bakery was the brainchild of Linda Haynes and her husband, Martin Connell—both keen amateur cooks who wanted to share their enthusiasm for handmade European-style rustic breads. The bakery opened in 1993 and simply took Toronto by storm. Today it supplies more than 250 restaurants, hotels and grocery stores as well as its own elegant café at the corner of Yonge Street and Balmoral.

Andrea Stewart joined the company as chef in December, 1998. A graduate of the Stratford Chefs School, she spent two years in New York before returning to Ontario to work at Mildred Pierce. It was there she created this recipe for artichoke tapenade, in collaboration with chef Claire Stubbs. Why the move to Ace? "I've always had a passion for bread," Stewart explains, "and I loved the idea of being in a bakery environment—a whole different ballgame from working the line in a restaurant kitchen."

WINE SUGGESTIONS
Ontario Sauvignon Blanc
Pouilly-Fumé (Loire Valley)
Sauvignon Blanc with its green, vegetal flavours is an ideal partner for artichoke.

Artichoke Tapenade

A simple recipe with lots of flavour, perfect to serve as a dip, on grilled bread or as an accompaniment to roast beef or grilled chicken sandwiches. Use roasted artichokes if you can find them, as they have much more flavour than the canned variety.

The tapenade should keep, refrigerated, for about one week.

---

2 cups canned artichokes, drained and quartered
1 cup pitted green olives
2 cloves garlic, chopped
1 tbsp green peppercorns in brine, drained
1 tbsp chopped anchovies

½ cup olive oil
¼ cup lemon juice
¼ cup chopped fresh oregano or 1 tbsp dried
¼ cup chopped fresh parsley
Salt and freshly ground pepper to taste

Puree artichokes, olives, garlic, peppercorns and anchovies in food processor. With machine running, gradually add oil and lemon juice through feed tube. Tapenade should be spreadable; if necessary, add more oil.

Stir in oregano and parsley. Season with salt and pepper.

Makes about 2 cups.

ACQUA

[ROB BUCHANAN]

Rob Buchanan only made up his mind to become a chef after he moved to Toronto from England fifteen years ago. His subsequent curriculum vitae reads like the A-list of the city's restaurants, including time at the Windsor Arms, at Scaramouche, at Bower's on Eglinton Avenue where he was co-chef with his wife, Suzanne Baby, and then a stint as chef of the Millcroft Inn. He came to cook at Acqua soon after Franco Prevedello opened the restaurant in the glass-and-steel forest of BCE Place's atrium. Three years ago, he and manager, Helder Carvalho, bought the business. "It needed a fair bit of fine tuning," remembers Buchanan. "We got rid of some of the pastas and pizzas and added the raw bar." Now the after-work crowd can feast on oysters and seafood, while the nearby Air Canada Centre has made the main dining room even busier whenever the Leafs or the Raptors play.

WINE SUGGESTIONS
Canadian Pinot Noir 🍁
Chianti (Tuscany) or Barbaresco (Piedmont)
The bitterness of arugula, the acidulous tomatoes and the earthiness of mushrooms suggest a red wine with good acidity.

Wild Mushrooms on Arugula Bruschetta

arugula bruschetta

This full-flavoured hors d'oeuvre is excellent before a dinner party. Use a combination of red and yellow tomatoes for eye appeal.

---

3 large tomatoes, seeded and chopped
¼ cup chopped fresh basil
¼ cup finely chopped red onion
1 tbsp balsamic vinegar
½ cup olive oil
4 cups coarsely chopped wild mushrooms

Salt and freshly ground pepper to taste
1 tbsp finely chopped garlic
1 baguette, cut on diagonal in ½-inch slices
1 bunch arugula, washed and stemmed
2½ tbsp white truffle oil (page 112)

Combine tomatoes, basil, onion, vinegar and ¼ cup olive oil in bowl.

Heat 2 tbsp olive oil in large skillet over medium-high heat. Add mushrooms and cook for 5 minutes, stirring occasionally, until liquid evaporates and mushrooms are golden and tender. Stir mushrooms into tomato mixture and season with salt and pepper.

Combine garlic with remaining 2 tbsp olive oil in small bowl. Brush over both sides of bread slices.

Grill bread on grill or under broiler for 2 minutes per side or until golden. Remove bread to platter.

Top bread with arugula and tomato-mushroom mixture. Drizzle with truffle oil.

Makes about 32.

THE AMAZING FOOD SERVICE [Andrew Zimbel]

"Have pots, will travel," was pretty much the motto of The Amazing Food Service when Andrew Zimbel created the one-man catering company in 1981. Though he was only twenty-three, he already had seven years' experience under his belt as a cook and waiter in Manitoba, Toronto and Prince Edward Island. His family had moved to a farm on P.E.I. from New York City when Andrew was in his teens, and he credits his passion for food to those years spent watching raw ingredients grow. Today, The Amazing Food Service is a full-service catering company, smoothly handling any kind of event from intimate dinner parties to corporate receptions for two thousand guests. Associated with Second Harvest since the organization began, Andrew was also co-chair of Taste '96, the year he prepared this terrific recipe.

WINE SUGGESTIONS
Canadian off-dry Riesling 🍁
German Riesling Spätlese
The sweetness of the potatoes, cream and crêpes calls for a white wine with some residual sugar.

CRÊPE TIPS

Crêpes are very versatile. They can be used in sweet or savoury dishes and can be made ahead of time and refrigerated for up to three days or frozen for up to one month. After crêpe batter has been made, it should stand for 30 minutes to 2 hours before cooking. The starch swells and is more easily broken down in cooking, resulting in a lighter, more tender crêpe.

The best crêpe pan is a non-stick, cast iron or cast aluminium pan. For thin, lacy crêpes, add only enough batter to barely cover the bottom of the pan.

Ginger Roasted Root Vegetable Roulades

The roasted vegetables and apples can also be served as a side dish with roast chicken or beef.

CRÊPES:
1½ cups all-purpose flour
1 tsp granulated sugar
¾ tsp salt
3 eggs
⅓ cup butter, melted
1½ cups milk
½ cup cold water
1 cup chopped fresh chives

FILLING:
2 beets, peeled
2 sweet potatoes, peeled
2 large parsnips, peeled
1 large onion, sliced
2 large tart apples, peeled and sliced
¼ cup chopped ginger
¼ cup vegetable oil
Salt and freshly ground pepper to taste
1 cup goat cheese
1 tbsp whipping cream
1 tbsp chopped fresh thyme

Whisk together flour, sugar, salt, eggs, melted butter and ¾ cup milk in large bowl or food processor. Whisk in remaining milk, water and chives until batter resembles thin syrup. Let batter stand for 30 minutes to 2 hours.

Preheat oven to 450°F. Cut beets, sweet potatoes and parsnips into sticks about ¼ inch thick.

Toss vegetables, apples, ginger, oil, salt and pepper. Spread in single layer on large rimmed baking sheet. Bake for 25 minutes or until tender.

Puree goat cheese, cream and thyme in food processor until smooth, adding more cream if needed.

Heat 9- or 10-inch lightly oiled non-stick skillet over medium heat. Pour in about ¼ cup batter to cover bottom of skillet. Cook just until bottom of crêpe is lightly browned, about 1 minute. Turn and cook for 30 to 45 seconds or until dry. Turn out onto plate. Repeat with remaining batter.

Place crêpe on counter and spread with 1 tbsp goat cheese mixture. Arrange some vegetables and apples along bottom third of crêpe and roll up firmly. Wrap in plastic wrap and refrigerate until firm. Repeat with remaining crêpes and filling.

Remove plastic wrap, cut crêpes diagonally into 1-inch lengths and arrange on platter.

Makes 64 pieces.

CAVIAR CENTRE

[M A R K   O M I D I]

You can hear the gasps of pleasure as people passing through Taste see Mark Omidi's display of fabulous Iranian caviar. Those who care to linger (and who doesn't?) will receive a gentle education in the fine points of the world's most expensive eggs, illustrated with tastes of matchless beluga, sevruga and osetra. While his company is not associated with any chef in particular, Omidi can call on the best in the city if some suave new caviar presentation is called for. "We are a family firm," he says. "I remember when I started the business in 1992. My first order was for two fifty-gram tins of sevruga. These days, hotels and restaurants often order ten kilos at a time. The city has become so sophisticated so quickly."

CAVIAR IDEAS

Prepare your favourite smoked salmon pasta and top with small mound of caviar to add flavour and colour.

Spoon out flesh from a boiled unpeeled baby potato. Combine potato flesh with sour cream and pinch finely chopped red onion. Stuff back into potato skin and top with caviar.

Make sushi rolls with rice and seaweed, cut in pieces and top with a few grains of caviar.

WINE SUGGESTIONS
If you want to wave the flag try a locally made sparkling wine. Otherwise, spoil yourself and go for the real thing — Champagne is the perfect companion for caviar.

Blini with Caviar and Crème Fraîche

An elegant hors d'oeuvre for that special occasion. Caviar comes in different qualities and different prices. The very best is beluga caviar—the eggs are bigger and the flavour bursts in your mouth. Osetra is the next best and sevruga, with its smaller eggs, is less expensive but still very good. Salmon caviar is a good buy for people who don't want the expense of sturgeon.

**12 blini or toasted brioche
or egg bread slices, buttered**
¼ cup crème fraîche (page 12) or sour cream

30 g beluga caviar
Lemon wedges

Arrange warm blini or toasts on tray.

Place small dollop of crème fraîche or sour cream on centre of each blini. Top with small spoonful of caviar and garnish with lemon wedges.

Makes 12 blini.

UNTRADITIONAL BLINI

For a quick blini that does not require yeast, in large bowl, combine 1 cup all-purpose flour, ⅓ cup buckwheat flour, 1 tsp baking powder and ½ tsp baking soda. In separate bowl, stir together 1 egg, pinch salt, pinch sugar, 1½ cups milk and 3 tbsp yogurt. Beat liquid ingredients into dry ingredients and let stand for 20 minutes.

Heat 2 tbsp butter in skillet on medium heat. Drop batter in skillet by scant tbsp and cook for about 30 seconds or until bubbles form on top and bottom is crisp. Turn and cook second side until golden, about 20 seconds.

Makes about 40.

ALLISON CUMMING

Allison Cumming has always had a passionate interest in cooking and food. After graduating from the School of Home Science at the University of Otago in New Zealand, and a brief teaching stint in Auckland, she set off across Asia and Europe, eventually reaching Oxford, England, where she taught for three years before opening her own catering business. Courses with John Toovey at Miller Howe in the Lake District, at Chez Hubert in Paris and with Paula Wolfert in New York added to her culinary repertoire, as did an advanced certificate from London's Cordon Bleu School of Cooking. In 1976, she moved to Toronto and opened her own catering company, which flourished for twenty years before Allison retired in 1996. She had always been a valiant supporter of Second Harvest; now she became involved with organizing Taste, most recently as chair of Taste '98 and co-chair of Taste '99. "I chose this recipe," she explains, "because I know that when busy people entertain they need some recipes that can be prepared ahead, cooked and served as easily as possible. Shrimp are always a big hit, and this recipe adds a new dimension to an old favourite."

WINE SUGGESTIONS
Ontario off-dry Riesling or BC Ehrenfelser 🍁
off-dry Vouvray (Loire)
Thai spicing screams out for a white wine with good fruit and some residual sweetness.

Warm Marinated Thai Shrimp

Marinate these ahead of time and pop them into the oven just before serving. You should get 10 to 15 jumbo shrimp to the pound. If you use smaller shrimp, reduce the baking time.

24 jumbo shrimp
½ cup lemon juice
¼ cup Thai fish sauce
¼ cup granulated sugar
1 tsp Asian chili sauce
2 tbsp grated ginger
3 cloves garlic, finely chopped

2 tbsp chopped fresh mint
2 tbsp chopped fresh coriander

GARNISH:
Lemon twists
2 tbsp chopped fresh coriander
2 tbsp chopped fresh mint

Peel and devein shrimp.

Combine lemon juice, fish sauce, sugar, chili sauce, ginger, garlic, 2 tbsp mint and 2 tbsp coriander in large bowl.

Add shrimp and toss with marinade. Cover and refrigerate for 8 to 24 hours.

Preheat oven to 350°F.

Place shrimp on toothpicks and arrange in single layer on baking sheet.

Bake shrimp until pink and slightly curled, 4 to 5 minutes. Garnish with lemon twists, chopped coriander and mint. Serve immediately.

Makes about 24.

DINAH'S CATERING AND
TIGER LILY'S NOODLE HOUSE   [DINAH KOO]

Hard to believe it's been twenty-five years since Dinah Koo opened her Cupboard on Cumberland Street and helped introduce this fair city to the notion of high-end prepared food—everything from yummy sandwiches to foie gras, from fresh herbs flown in from France to the blend of coffee beans created for Fenton's restaurant. Dinah eventually sold the store (which still flourishes) to concentrate on catering, and then started her noodle house, bringing Toronto another idea—that simple Asian street food can be wonderful when it is beautifully prepared with first-class ingredients.

CRÈME FRAÎCHE

Combine 2 parts whipping cream and 1 part sour cream. Cover and let rest at room temperature for 24 hours or until thick.

WINE SUGGESTIONS
Canadian dry Gewürztraminer or Muscat 🍁
Alsace Gewürztraminer
The spicing calls for an aromatic white wine like Gewürztraminer. If you can't find Gerwürz, go for a dry Riesling.

BEER SUGGESTION
Belgian white beer
A wonderful hors d'oeuvre deserves a great aperitif beer. The coriander used in the brewing of this white beer will play off the dipping sauce nicely.

Chicken Dumplings with Spicy Coriander Sauce

These are wonderful make-ahead hors d'oeuvre. Cook, refrigerate overnight and reheat on a baking sheet in a 350°F oven for 5 minutes. If you can't find kimch'i, use 1 tsp Asian chili sauce; if you can't find dumpling skins, use wonton wrappers.

SPICY CORIANDER SAUCE:
2 tsp cornstarch
1 cup chicken stock, cold
1 cup fresh coriander leaves
1 tbsp grated ginger
1 tsp finely chopped garlic
1½ to 2 tsp Asian chili sauce
Salt to taste
¼ cup crème fraîche (page 12) or sour cream

FILLING:
1 lb boneless skinless chicken breasts
1 tbsp soy sauce
1 tsp mirin (Japanese rice wine)
½ tsp finely chopped garlic
½ cup coarsely chopped shiitake mushrooms
½ cup corn kernels
¼ cup coarsely chopped kimch'i (page 28)
½ cup coarsely chopped canned bamboo shoots
¼ cup chopped green onions
1 tbsp oyster sauce
Salt to taste
1 package dumpling wrappers

Dissolve cornstarch in chicken stock in small saucepan. Bring to boil over medium-high heat, stirring until stock has thickened. Cool slightly and pour into blender or food processor.

Add coriander, ginger, 1 tsp garlic, chili sauce, salt and crème fraîche; process until smooth. Reserve.

Chop chicken coarsely and transfer to large bowl. Add soy sauce, mirin and ½ tsp garlic; let stand for 20 minutes.

Stir in mushrooms, corn, kimch'i, bamboo shoots, green onions, oyster sauce and salt.

Place single dumpling wrapper on work surface. Moisten ½ inch of outer edge with water. Place 1 tsp filling in centre, fold in half and press edges to seal well. Repeat with remaining wrappers and filling.

Boil water in large saucepan. Drop in dumplings 8 to 10 at a time. Cook for about 3 to 4 minutes or until dumplings float to surface and wrappers appear translucent. Lift out with slotted spoon and drain well. Serve immediately with dipping sauce.

Makes about 50 dumplings.

EDO

[DAVID CHUNG]

A Montreal native, Barry Chaim knew next to nothing about Japan when he first went there in 1972 on a graduate research fellowship in psychology from the University of Tokyo. But he learned quickly, especially after forming an import company that dealt with far eastern suppliers. In partnership with two Japanese friends, he opened Edo restaurant on Eglinton West in 1987, but only began to take an active interest nine years later when his partners moved on. Since then, Edo has gone from strength to strength, giving birth to a second restaurant, Edo-ko in Forest Hill Village and playing a very successful supporting role at the Air Canada Centre. Under executive chef David Chung, the menu is classically Japanese, subtly laced with creative innovations such as the awesome and irresistible Dynamite Roll. Meanwhile, Barry Chaim has become an eloquent ambassador for his adopted cuisine, and an expert in finding the ideal beer, sake or wine for the little masterpieces that emerge from the kitchen and sushi bar.

KONBU

Konbu is sea kelp and is used in making dashi (Japanese fish stock) and for flavouring sushi rice. You can buy it in sheets or in shredded form. Don't wash konbu, as rinsing will remove the flavour.

WINE SUGGESTIONS
Ontario off-dry Riesling ❧
German Riesling Spätlese
Matched to the pickled ginger and wasabi, both powerful flavours.

California Rolls nori

California rolls made sushi acceptable—easy to make and not beyond the abilities of the home cook. Use medium-grain Japanese rice; you need the starch to hold the rice together. A bamboo mat will also make rolling easier. Garnish the serving platter with pickled ginger, wasabi and soy sauce.

SUSHI RICE:
2½ cups Japanese rice
3½ cups cold water
⅓ cup rice vinegar
2 tbsp granulated sugar
2 tbsp shredded konbu, or 2-inch square sheet,
　　finely chopped
Salt to taste

SUSHI ROLLS:
5 sheets nori
7 oz cooked crab meat
⅓ cup flying fish roe (tobiko) or smelt roe
1 avocado, thinly sliced
½ English cucumber, peeled and cut in
　　long thin strips
3 green onions, green part only, cut in thin strips

Place rice in heavy saucepan with cold water. Cover and bring to boil. Reduce heat and simmer, covered, for 25 minutes or until water is absorbed and rice is tender. Transfer rice to large bowl.

Combine vinegar, sugar, konbu and salt in separate saucepan. Cook over medium heat, stirring, until sugar dissolves.

Pour vinegar mixture over cooked rice and mix together gently. Cover with damp tea towel and cool.

Place sheet of nori on bamboo mat or tea towel. Using slightly damp hands, spread thin layer of rice over nori, leaving ½-inch border. Starting at bottom end of nori, place some crab, roe, avocado, cucumber and green onion over rice.

Roll up nori tightly. Repeat with remaining ingredients.

Cut each roll in half. Line up halves and cut together in thirds.

Makes 30 pieces.

IL FORNELLO [IAN SORBIE AND TONY RAGO]

Ian Sorbie opened his first Il Fornello in 1986, in the Bloor-Bathurst area. Today there are ten, including one franchise in Saint John, New Brunswick, and two more will soon be appearing at the airport. What has been the secret of Sorbie's success? Perhaps it is simply that people loved the innovative opportunity to invent their own pizza from a choice of fifty toppings. Or maybe we just love the crisp, flavourful crust of a pizza baked in a wood-burning oven (Il Fornello's trademark ovens were almost the first in the city). As for the recipes— "We've always been a very collaborative company," says Sorbie, "and if someone comes up with a good idea, we use it." Among those ideas are soy milk cappuccino, pizzas with gluten-free amaranth crusts for celiacs or with spelt crusts for people with candida. Now everyone can enjoy one of the best pizzas in town.

WINE SUGGESTIONS
Canadian Gamay Noir 🍁
Chianti (Tuscany) or Valpolicella (Veneto)
Whenever tomato sauce is involved, look for a light red wine with good acidity.

QUICK TOMATO SAUCE

Heat 2 tbsp olive oil in skillet over medium-high heat. Add 1 chopped clove garlic and 1 chopped onion. Cook for 3 minutes until onion is translucent. Add 1 28-oz/796 mL can tomatoes, chopped up with their liquid, 2 tbsp tomato paste, 1 bay leaf and 1 tsp dried oregano. Bring to a boil, reduce heat and simmer, uncovered, until thickened, about 15 minutes. Season well with salt and pepper. Remove bay leaf and discard.

Makes about 2 cups.

Pizza with Tomato Sauce

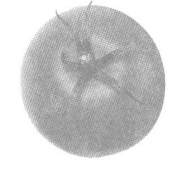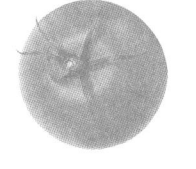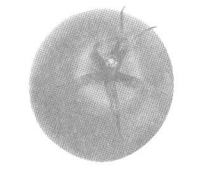

This appetizing crust is crisp on the outside and tender inside. Vary the toppings using different cheeses, vegetables, spices, sausage or prosciutto.

⅔ cup warm water	1½ tsp salt
1 tsp granulated sugar	1 cup tomato sauce (page 16)
2 tsp active dry yeast	1 cup grated mozzarella cheese
1½ cups all-purpose flour	¼ cup grated Parmesan cheese

Combine water and sugar in large bowl. Sprinkle yeast over surface and mix with fork until yeast and sugar have dissolved. Let stand in warm place for 10 to 15 minutes until frothy.

Sift flour and salt into large mixing bowl. Pour in yeast mixture. Lightly oil or flour your hands and work flour and liquid together into a ball.

Knead dough on generously floured work surface until soft and supple, about 5 minutes. If dough is too dry, add warm water ½ tsp at a time. If dough is too wet, add flour 1 tsp at a time until dough is no longer sticky.

Place dough in lightly floured bowl, cover bowl with damp cloth and let stand in warm place for about 1 hour. Dough should double in volume.

Preheat oven to 450°F. Lightly oil or flour your hands. Lift dough from underneath and punch it down. Divide into two pieces. Form each into smooth round ball. Cover and let rest for 10 to 15 minutes.

Stretch or roll each ball into 10-inch circle. Place on pizza pans and top with tomato sauce, mozzarella and Parmesan.

Bake on bottom shelf of oven for 7 to 8 minutes or until edges are crusty and brown.

Makes 2 pizzas.

GRAND YATT DYNASTY [DAVID LUK]

There are two menus at this handsome restaurant tucked into the Westin Harbour Castle Hotel—one in English and one in Cantonese. They seem to refer to different cuisines—the first full of sweet retro Chinese Canadian dishes, the second one far more interesting. This is the card to read for seasonal specialties, succulent seafood, crispy-skinned orange chicken and five-snake soup, lovingly prepared by chef Kwok Wong. This Sichuan recipe was prepared for Taste '97 by chef David Luk.

SOY GINGER DIPPING SAUCE

Mix together ¼ cup soy sauce, ⅓ cup rice vinegar, 1 tsp grated ginger and 2 chopped green onions.

WINE SUGGESTIONS
Ontario off-dry Riesling 🍁
Germany's Rheingau Riesling Spätlese
A spicy, hot dish requires a white wine with a touch of sweetness.

BEER SUGGESTION
Czech-style pilsner
Spicy, deep-fried food needs a crisp, hoppy beer to cleanse the palate and assuage the heat.

Sichuan Spring Rolls

Sichuan means spicy, and these rolls can be as hot as you like. You can also use twenty large spring roll wrappers and cut each one in half to serve. Serve with the soy ginger dipping sauce (page 18).

---

1 cup dried Chinese mushrooms	1 tbsp Asian chili sauce, or to taste
1 cup hot water	2 tsp sesame oil
1 lb lean ground pork	Salt to taste
1 tbsp grated ginger	3 tbsp cornstarch
1 cup chopped canned bamboo shoots	1 tbsp cold water
1 tbsp granulated sugar	3 egg yolks
1 tbsp oyster sauce	40 5-inch spring roll wrappers
2 tbsp soy sauce	Vegetable oil for deep-frying

Cover mushrooms with hot water and soak for 20 minutes or until soft. Drain, reserving mushroom water. Remove stems and slice mushrooms.

Combine pork, ginger, bamboo shoots and mushrooms in skillet on medium-high heat. Add mushroom-soaking liquid. Bring to boil and simmer until pork is no longer pink, about 5 minutes.

Add sugar, oyster sauce, soy sauce, chili sauce and sesame oil. Season with salt if necessary. Mixture should be highly seasoned. Cook, stirring, until well combined.

Increase heat to high. Combine 1 tbsp cornstarch and 1 tbsp cold water and stir into mixture. Cook, stirring, until thickened. Remove from heat and let cool to room temperature.

Mix together egg yolks and remaining 2 tbsp cornstarch in small bowl.

Place single spring roll wrapper on counter with point toward you. Place 1½ tbsp pork mixture in centre of wrapper. Brush edges with egg yolk mixture. Fold in three corners and then roll up. Place on baking sheet seam side down. Repeat with remaining wrappers.

Heat oil in wok or deep fryer on medium-high heat. Add spring rolls a few at a time and fry for about 2 minutes or until golden. Drain on paper towels.

Makes about 40 pieces.

HIRO SUSHI

[HIRO YOSHIDA]

BONITO

Bonito is a member of the mackerel family. The mackerel is dried and then shaved into flakes. It is one of the basic ingredients in making dashi (Japanese soup stock) and is available at Asian markets.

Hiro Yoshida has many fans. Toronto's top chefs revere him. Corporate demiurges visiting from Japan ask humbly for his personal services when an important dinner is to be prepared. Tall, dignified and courteous, he is a traditionalist where sushi is concerned, unimpressed by the extravagant innovations of fusion artistes. A graduate in international economics from Takushoku University in Tokyo, he began his long apprenticeship as a sushi chef later than most. In 1983, his training complete, he came to Toronto and has lived here ever since.

It is every sushi chef's dream to have a restaurant of his own. Yoshida opened Hiro Sushi on Church Street in 1990, with Meiko Kimura as his kitchen chef. In 1998 they moved to less austere premises on King Street West. His regular clientele followed en masse, loath to give up the intimate relationship that evolves between a sushi master and his customers.

WINE SUGGESTIONS
Canadian off-dry Riesling 🍁
Alsace Tokay-Pinot Gris or California Viognier
A sweet and sour dressing calls for the same character in a wine—lively acidity and a touch of fruity sweetness.

Japanese Citrus Dressing (Ponzu Sauce)

citrus dressing

A traditional Japanese dipping sauce for sashimi, sunomono and one-pot dishes such as shabu shabu.

---

1 cup soy sauce
¼ cup lemon juice
¼ cup lime juice
¼ cup orange juice

¼ cup rice vinegar
½ cup water
1 2-inch square konbu (page 14)
2 tbsp bonito flakes

Combine soy sauce, lemon, lime and orange juices, vinegar and water in bowl. Add konbu and bonito flakes. Cover and refrigerate overnight.

Strain mixture; discard konbu and bonito. Store dressing in refrigerator for up to 3 months.

Makes 2¼ cups.

JK ROM

[JAMIE KENNEDY]

The greater the chef, the greater the French fry. As a maxim, this proposition may not always hold true, but it was gloriously borne out at Taste '98. Nineteen years have passed since Jamie Kennedy, barely out of his teens, opened Scaramouche and became our first home-grown celebrity chef. Since then he has given us Palmerston, cooked at the Founder's Club inside SkyDome, and for the past six years has exhibited his tremendous talents in his own restaurant at the Royal Ontario Museum. But for Kennedy, food is about more than just cooking, and celebrity brings more than just an adoring clientele. As one of the founders of Knives and Forks, he has used his status to pioneer an appreciation for the manifold virtues of organic produce, while his work with Empty Bowls has helped to raise public awareness of urban poverty. And, of course, he has proved a most valiant supporter of Second Harvest.

WINE SUGGESTIONS
Canadian non-oaked Chardonnay 🍁
Chablis or Rhône white
A crisp, dry white to offset the fried potatoes and the saltiness of the squid.

French Fries and Squid with Olive Mayonnaise

The famous Kennedy French fries for the home cook. The first frying blanches the potatoes and cooks them through without colouring. The second frying at a higher temperature crisps them. (You can do the first frying earlier in the day, but do not refrigerate the potatoes.)

The squid adds depth to an already terrific dish. Serve as a nibble in paper cones, or as a side dish.

¼ cup pitted black olives
2 cloves garlic
1 tbsp lemon juice
1 tsp anchovy paste
Pinch salt
1 cup mayonnaise

Vegetable oil for deep-frying
1 lb Yukon Gold potatoes, peeled and
    cut in ⅛-inch sticks
Sea salt to taste
1 lb squid, cut in rings ¼ inch thick
1 cup all-purpose flour

Combine olives, garlic, lemon juice, anchovy paste and salt in food processor. Puree until smooth. Transfer to small bowl and stir in mayonnaise.

Heat oil in deep-fryer or deep, heavy saucepan to 300°F (or until cube of bread turns brown in 30 seconds). In batches, fry potatoes for 3 to 5 minutes or just until tender but not brown; place on baking sheet to cool.

Increase oil temperature to 375°F (or until bread cube turns brown in 15 seconds). In batches, fry potatoes for 2 to 3 min-utes or until golden-brown and crisp. Drain on paper towels; sprinkle with sea salt.

Dredge squid rings in flour, shaking off excess. Deep-fry in batches for 1 to 2 minutes or until golden-brown and crisp. Drain on paper towels; sprinkle with sea salt.

Roll 8½ x 11-inch sheets of brown paper into cones. Fill with potatoes and squid. Top with dollop of olive mayonnaise.

Makes 16 servings.

LAI WAH HEEN

Look around the chic dining room of Lai Wah Heen at lunchtime and chances are you will see a scattering of Toronto's leading chefs quietly enjoying the city's most elegant dim sum. Henry Wu aimed for the top when he decided to create a Cantonese restaurant in the Metropolitan Hotel, a room to rival the great hotel restaurants in Hong Kong. He decorated the space with smart pastel colours and sweeping sight lines. Then he brought in chef Ken Tam and built him a kitchen that would meet his every need. Can food be simultaneously decadent and disciplined? It can at Lai Wah Heen.

WINE SUGGESTIONS
Canadian Chardonnay 🍁
New Zealand Chardonnay
The pancakes add a softness to the flavour of the lobster so choose a Chardonnay
from a cool growing region (the wine will have good acidity).

Cantonese-style Lobster Pancakes

lobster pancakes

You can use shrimp or scallops instead of lobster in these pancakes. The glutinous rice flour gives the pancake a slightly chewy texture and crisp coating; it is available in Asian grocery stores.

1 cup glutinous rice flour	**¼ cup finely diced sweet green pepper**
¾ cup all-purpose flour	**¼ cup finely diced sweet red pepper**
1½ cups water	**½ cup finely diced onion**
6 shiitake mushroom caps, finely diced	**Salt and freshly ground pepper to taste**
1 cup chopped cooked lobster meat (about 4 oz)	**3 tbsp vegetable oil**

Combine rice flour and all-purpose flour in bowl. Whisk in enough water to give mixture consistency of pancake batter.

Stir in mushrooms, lobster, sweet peppers, onion, salt and pepper.

Heat 1 tbsp oil in 9-inch non-stick skillet on medium heat. Pour in one-third of batter. Cook for about 3 minutes per side or until golden-brown and crisp. Set aside and keep warm. Repeat with remaining oil and batter to make 3 large pancakes. Cut each pancake into 6 wedges.

Makes 18 pieces

LOTUS

AVOCADOS

Haas avocados grow in California, and they have purplish-black, pebbly skins. The flesh is rich and buttery and is said to have a superior flavour to other species. The fat content of Haas avocados is also slightly lower than that of the smooth-skinned variety.

Born and raised in Hong Kong, trained in classical European cuisine at the famous Peninsula Hotel in Kowloon, Susur Lee came to Toronto in 1978, where he soon became part of the hip food scene on Queen Street West. There could scarcely be a more discordant trio of influences, but Susur turned them into beautiful music when he opened Lotus in 1986. For the next ten years, the ascetic little room on an unfashionable side street became a place of pilgrimage for all who loved brilliant cooking. While other fusion chefs played with multicultural ingredients, Susur worked at a deeper, more instinctive level, balancing the yin and yang of elements on every plate. Prowling the Food Terminal at dawn, he sought out what was fresh and inspiring, then brought his inimitable imagination to bear, dazzling the city with his technique, delighting us with his wit and his integrity. Who else could turn a couple of broccoli stalks into something unrecognizably crisp, succulent and delicious? Who else would even have thought to try?

WINE SUGGESTIONS
BC Pinot Gris ❧
California Sauvignon Blanc
Tuna is a meaty fish that needs a white wine with a touch of sweetness.

Pounded Tuna with Avocado and Wasabi Compote and Chinese Taro Crisps

Taro, a dry-fleshed Asian vegetable, can be hard to find; substitute Yukon Gold potatoes. This can also be served in a small savoury tuile (page 49) for a spectacular presentation.

1 small Haas avocado, finely diced
4 tsp finely chopped shallot
1 tbsp lemon juice
1½ tsp crème fraîche (page 12)
   or mayonnaise
½ tsp wasabi paste

8 oz sushi-quality tuna
1 tbsp soy sauce
1 tsp olive oil
Salt and freshly ground pepper to taste
Vegetable oil for deep-frying
2 taro or Yukon Gold potatoes

Combine avocado, 3 tsp shallot, lemon juice, crème fraîche and wasabi paste in bowl.

Slice tuna into rounds ⅜ inch thick. Place slices between layers of plastic wrap and pound until ⅛ inch thick.

Mince tuna finely and place in bowl. Add soy sauce, oil, remaining 1 tsp shallot, salt and pepper.

Heat several inches of vegetable oil to 375°F (or until bread cube turns brown in 15 seconds) in wok or deep saucepan.

Peel taro and cut into slices ⅛ inch thick. Fry slices in batches for 3 to 5 minutes or until golden, crisp and cooked through. Drain on paper towels and sprinkle with salt.

Top each taro slice with ½ tsp avocado mixture and 1½ tsp tuna mixture.

Makes about 20.

MERCER STREET GRILL [Renée Foote]

Remember the mid-1990s, when the homespun, post-recession fad for mashed potatoes and gravy threatened to drag many Toronto menus back to the Diefenbaker years? Renée Foote's highly individual Asian-fusion cooking was always the heavenly antidote, especially when she joined Simon Bower's delightful little restaurant on Mercer Street. The plate or bento box would arrive at the table, the presentation often unabashedly vertical, merry with noodle antennae or dots of nori made with a hole-punch—witty, outrageous, but so good to eat. And chocolate sushi to finish. Mashed potatoes and gravy have slipped back to their humble but worthy place on the ground floor of the palace of gastronomy. Although Renée Foote is no longer at Mercer Street Grill, her cooking continues to dance nimbly over the rooftops through her catering company, Ginger Island.

KIMCH'I

Kimch'i is a fiery combination of chilies and garlic fermented with Chinese cabbage. Although in Korea it sometimes replaces vegetables during winter months, it is usually served as a condiment.

WINE SUGGESTIONS
BC Syrah ❧
California Zinfandel or Australian Shiraz
The marinade and sauce determine the style of wine required: a robust, full-bodied red with oodles of fruit extract.

Steamer Buns of Barbecued Beef Tenderloin with Korean Flavours

Serve with kimch'i as an hors d'oeuvre or as part of an Asian meal. The buns can also be purchased in the freezer section of Asian supermarkets (resteam before using), or you can omit the buns and serve the beef with stir-fried spinach and sticky rice as a main course.

---

3 tbsp sesame oil
3 tbsp vegetable oil
4 cloves garlic, finely chopped
1 tbsp Asian chili sauce
1 lb beef tenderloin

GREEN ONION BUNS:
2¼ cups all-purpose flour
¼ cup granulated sugar
4 tsp baking powder
½ tsp salt

3 green onions, chopped
⅓ cup milk
¼ cup water
4 tsp vegetable oil

BARBECUE SAUCE:
½ cup oyster sauce
1 tbsp Asian fish sauce
1 tbsp brown sugar
1½ tsp lime juice
¾ tsp coarsely ground pepper

Whisk together sesame and vegetable oils, garlic and chili sauce in small bowl. Place beef in baking dish; pour marinade over and turn to coat. Cover and refrigerate for 8 to 12 hours. Bring to room temperature before grilling.

Combine flour, sugar, baking powder, salt and green onions in large bowl. Stir in milk, water and oil to form a ragged dough. Knead for 10 minutes or until dough springs back when poked. Place dough in bowl; cover and let stand for 1 hour.

Roll dough into 16 balls. Place 1 inch apart in steamer over simmering water. Cover and steam for 10 minutes.

Whisk together oyster sauce, fish sauce, brown sugar, lime juice and pepper in bowl.

Remove beef from marinade. Whisk barbecue sauce into remaining marinade. Brush meat with marinade and place on grill over high heat. Close lid and grill for 15 to 20 minutes or until rare, turning once and brushing with marinade during cooking. Let stand for 10 minutes before slicing thinly. Slice buns in half horizontally and fill with warm sliced beef.

Makes 16.

MONSOON

[B R A D   M O O R E]

MISO

Miso is a fermented soybean paste with a fragrant, slightly salty taste. Light or yellow miso is the mildest and is used to flavour soups, sauces and vegetables. Dark red or brown miso is used in heartier soups, vegetable and bean dishes.

New Asian... that was the term Brad Moore always used to describe his cuisine at Monsoon. The menu was drawn from that part of the world where the monsoon falls—from Japan to the Himalayas. A substantial slice of the planet, but Moore took only the most judicious liberties with his generous mandate. Clarity, subtlety and self-discipline characterized his dishes, and the cultural cross-overs all made perfect sense the moment one began to eat. Happily, his philosophy was also broad enough to encompass a wry wit. The tuna spring rolls he prepared at Taste '98 delighted everyone with their presentation as well as with their delicious flavour—he served each one with a pair of chopsticks in a wee cardboard box. Hip, elegant, urban and exotic, Moore's cooking found a perfect setting at Monsoon, which beat out several multi-million-dollar New York restaurants to win the James Beard Foundation's 1998 Outstanding Restaurant Design award—the first time a Canadian establishment had even been nominated. Now Brad has moved on, but Monsoon's kitchen continues to cook up a storm. Long may it rain.

WINE SUGGESTIONS
BC Kerner or Ontario Scheurebe ❧
Alsace dry Muscat or German Riesling Kabinett
To match the spiciness, an aromatic white wine with a touch of residual sweetness.

BEER SUGGESTION
Saké
Made from fermented grain, saké is technically a beer. A good quality saké served chilled will accentuate each of the diverse flavours in this dish.

Yellowfin Tuna Rolls with Miso-Sesame and Wasabi-Tangerine Paints

There are many steps to this recipe but the final result tastes and looks great. You can omit the paints if you wish.

Togarishi is a very hot Japanese pepper mix. If you can't find it, substitute a pinch of cayenne.

MISO-SESAME PAINT:
1 tbsp light miso paste
1 tbsp sesame oil
¼ cup mirin (Japanese rice wine)
3 tbsp rice vinegar

WASABI-TANGERINE PAINT:
2 tbsp wasabi powder
2 tbsp mirin (Japanese rice wine)
½ cup fresh tangerine or orange juice

TUNA ROLLS:
16 rice paper wrappers
1 package enoki mushrooms, lower stems removed
1 cup finely diced shiitake mushroom caps
8 fresh chives, cut in half
1 small carrot, cut in julienne strips 3 inches long
1 tsp togarishi pepper
1 lb yellowfin tuna, cut in 16 strips
4 sheets nori, cut in 16 strips
2 tbsp sesame oil

Combine miso and sesame oil in small bowl. Gradually add ¼ cup mirin and vinegar, whisking constantly.

Whisk together wasabi powder, 2 tbsp mirin and tangerine juice in separate small bowl.

Soak rice paper wrapper in bowl of warm water for 1 minute. Shake off excess water and lay wrapper on flat surface. Place 4 enoki mushrooms, 1 tbsp shiitake mushrooms, chive piece, carrot strip, pinch pepper, tuna strip and nori strip just below centre of wrapper.

Fold bottom edge over filling. Fold in both sides and roll up tightly. Repeat with remaining wrappers and filling. Brush rolls with sesame oil.

Oil rolls lightly and cook on grill over medium-high heat for 1 minute per side. Place rolls on plate drizzled with miso-sesame and wasabi-tangerine paints.

Makes 16 rolls.

360 REVOLVING RESTAURANT   [PETER GEORGE]

The tallest restaurant. The highest wine cellar outside an airplane. Numbers—two thousand meals on a busy day—to flabbergast the average kitchen. Revolving restaurants had always had a dubious reputation in Toronto, but chef Brad Long from Pronto and manager Alfred Caron from Bistro 990 were determined to change all that when they took over 360, the huge circular room at the top of the CN Tower. Service would be suave, personal, well informed; the extraordinary wine list would encompass the best of Ontario alongside four-figure masterpieces. And Brad Long's menus reached as high. Here was ostrich gravlax with white truffle oil, baby octopus zuppa, excellent venison, and the desserts were always deliciously innovative. Now Long has found a new challenge as executive chef at the Air Canada Centre, leaving the great kitchen in the sky in the experienced hands of Peter George.

WINE SUGGESTIONS
Canadian barrel-fermented Chardonnay 🍁
Vernaccia di San Gimignano (Tuscany) or chilled Retsina (Greece)
A dry, white wine with definite personality to stand up to the salty, smoky flavours.

Smoked Eggplant in Mini Pitas with Green Olive Salsa

The smoky eggplant puree contrasts nicely with the sharpness of the salsa. Instead of mini pitas you could cut large pitas into wedges and serve the eggplant and the salsa as dips.

Use round Sicilian eggplant in this dish if you can; it is sweeter than the regular kind and doesn't have to be salted.

---

1 large eggplant
Salt and freshly ground pepper to taste
¼ cup roasted garlic puree (page 94)
Pinch cayenne
1 tbsp olive oil
1 tbsp lemon juice
32 mini pitas

GREEN OLIVE SALSA:
1 tbsp chopped fresh basil
¼ cup olive oil
1 tbsp capers
1 cup pitted sliced green olives
1 tsp grated lemon rind

Preheat barbecue and turn to low heat. Soak large handful of hickory wood chips and place on barbecue; close lid.

Cut eggplant in half horizontally and sprinkle cut sides with salt. When wood chips have started to smoke, place eggplant flesh down on barbecue. Close lid and cook for 15 minutes. Turn and cook skin side down for 15 minutes longer or until eggplant is cooked through and flesh is very soft. Cool.

Scoop eggplant flesh into bowl. Add roasted garlic, cayenne, 1 tbsp oil, lemon juice, salt and pepper. Blend together well.

Place basil, ¼ cup oil, capers, olives and lemon rind in food processor and pulse until mixed but not pureed.

Grill mini pitas for 30 seconds per side. Stuff with eggplant and top with salsa.

Makes 32 pieces.

First Courses

ACCENTS

[Nigel Didcock]

Calm, uncluttered, offering imaginative, beautifully prepared food at a very reasonable price, Accents is the very model of a modern hotel restaurant. Executive chef Nigel Didcock has always been swift to share the credit with his team, but it is his mind and his meticulous eye for detail that turns every corner of the menu into a delicious event. An Englishman, Didcock trained at The Connaught Hotel in London, a great bastion of classical French and English cuisine, before embarking on a long sojourn in France that included a year as chef-saucier at the legendary Troisgros. He was twenty-five when he came to Canada to open Langdon Hall's kitchen, championing local produce and making magic out of the bounty of the hotel's vegetable garden. Arriving at Sutton Place, his first task was to drag the hotel's dining room into the modern era, dispensing with pomp, creating a new restaurant of clean-cut elegance. "It's a team effort," repeats Didcock; but every team needs a leader.

Wine Suggestions
BC Pinot Blanc or Ontario Chardonnay ☀
white Burgundy
A well-balanced white wine will set off the creamy texture of the sweetbreads.
Use the same wine in the preparation of the dish.

Grilled Sweetbreads

Sweetbreads come from the pancreas and thymus gland of veal or lamb. They are delicate and soft, but grilling gives them a firmer texture than other cooking methods. Their great advantage is that they absorb flavours—a rich sauce or herbal marinade can make them burst with taste.

---

8 oz veal sweetbreads
1 cup water
½ cup dry white wine
1 carrot, chopped
1 onion, chopped
1 stalk celery, chopped

2 tsp chopped fresh thyme
2 tsp chopped fresh rosemary
¼ cup olive oil
2 tbsp balsamic vinegar
12 medium-sized shiitake mushroom caps
Salt and freshly ground pepper to taste

Soak sweetbreads overnight in cold water. Drain and rinse well.

Combine water, wine, carrot, onion, celery, 1 tsp thyme and 1 tsp rosemary in saucepan. Bring to boil. Add sweetbreads. Reduce heat to medium and simmer for 15 minutes. Drain and cool slightly. Remove any membranes or sinews.

Place sweetbreads on plate. Cover with second plate weighted down with cans and leave for 1 hour. Discard any liquid. Cut sweetbreads into twelve 1-inch cubes.

Whisk together oil, vinegar, remaining thyme and rosemary in large bowl. Add shiitakes and sweetbreads to marinade and turn to coat. Marinate for 30 minutes.

Soak 4 wooden skewers in water for 20 minutes.

Thread mushrooms onto soaked skewers alternately with sweetbreads, reserving marinade.

Brush mushrooms and sweetbreads lightly with oil and place on grill over medium-high heat. Close lid and grill for 5 minutes, turning once and brushing several times with remaining marinade. Sprinkle with salt and pepper.

Makes 4 servings.

APPETIZINGLY YOURS

[JIM LOAT AND INGRID VON CUBE]

Appetizingly Yours has grown from a small home business designing private parties to a full-service caterer serving personal and large corporate events all over Ontario and as far away as Nova Scotia. Chef Jim Loat began his career working in several restaurants in the Winnipeg area before moving to Guelph to study food science and commerce. He joined Appetizingly Yours in 1991. A keen believer in using fresh local ingredients whenever possible, he particularly enjoys working with the fresh herbs, flowers and produce harvested from the company's own organic garden.

WINE SUGGESTIONS
Canadian Sauvignon Blanc 🍁
Sancerre (Loire) or Soave (Veneto)
The crisp, green fruit and grassy flavours of Sauvignon Blanc work well with goat cheese and summer vegetables.

CHÈVRE SAGE BUTTER

Blend together ¼ cup soft goat cheese and 2 tbsp butter. Stir in 2 tsp chopped fresh sage. Season with pepper to taste.

Makes about ⅓ cup.

Grilled Polenta with Chèvre Sage Butter and Roasted Vegetables

chèvre sage butter

Change the vegetables according to the season, using squash, sweet potatoes, onions and rutabaga in winter and zucchini, eggplant, peppers and tomatoes in summer.

POLENTA:
3 cups vegetable stock or water
2 tsp salt
1 cup cornmeal
2 tbsp butter

ROASTED VEGETABLES:
4 cups assorted seasonal vegetables,
   cut in 1-inch cubes
2 tbsp olive oil
2 tbsp chopped fresh rosemary or 2 tsp dried
Salt and freshly ground pepper to taste

SUN-DRIED TOMATO ROASTED GARLIC VINAIGRETTE:
¼ cup sun-dried tomatoes
2 tbsp roasted garlic puree (page 94)
3 tbsp red wine vinegar
½ cup olive oil
Salt and freshly ground pepper to taste

⅓ cup chèvre sage butter (page 38)

Bring stock and salt to boil in heavy saucepan. In slow, steady stream, add cornmeal, stirring constantly. Reduce heat to medium and cook, stirring constantly, until mixture is thickened and pulls away from sides of pan, about 5 to 30 minutes depending on type of cornmeal used. Remove from heat and stir in 2 tbsp butter. Pour into lightly oiled 8-inch square pan and smooth top. Refrigerate until set, 2 hours or overnight.

Preheat oven to 450°F. Combine vegetables, 2 tbsp oil, rosemary, salt and pepper in roasting pan in single layer. Roast for 25 to 30 minutes or until browned and tender.

Cover sun-dried tomatoes with boiling water and let stand for 20 minutes or until softened. Drain.

Puree roasted garlic, drained tomatoes and vinegar in food processor. With motor running, gradually add ½ cup oil through feed tube. Season with salt and pepper.

Cut polenta into slices ½ inch thick. Brush lightly with oil and place on preheated grill on medium heat. Cook until heated and grill-marked, turning once. Spread with chèvre sage butter.

Toss vegetables with vinaigrette and spoon over polenta.

Makes 4 servings.

AVALON

[CHRIS McDONALD]

When is a chef ready to take that alarming step out of somebody else's restaurant and open a place of his own? For Chris McDonald the moment of commitment came in 1995, when he created Avalon. His training had begun as a teenager, sixteen years earlier, had progressed to the frantic, fascinating kitchen of Stadtländer's and included long stints in Mexico, Italy and the U.S. At Santa Fe and Massimo Rosticceria, he had won the plaudits of the media, but it was Avalon that set him among Toronto's culinary elite. He knows his wines as well as any chef in the city. A dinner there is a chamber sonata, each dish scored for three or four perfectly harmonious flavours, and while his sauces can be profound, even exotic, he is wise enough to let fabulous ingredients speak for themselves. Whenever possible, those ingredients come from local organic farms, but Chris has also been known to move mountains to bring in special treats such as the extraordinary Copper River salmon from Alaska that draws gourmets to his tables like wasps to jam.

Wine Suggestions
BC Pinot Blanc or Ontario Pinot Blanc 🍁
Chablis (Burgundy)
The cream adds a little sweetness so choose a white wine with a good fruit extract.

SALT COD

Salt cod is preserved fish; traditionally the cod was salted and sun dried to be used by sailors and travellers on long journeys. It is used in many traditional Mediterranean dishes, including *brandade de morue*, a provençale mixture of salt cod and potatoes. The cod must be soaked and drained before using to remove the salt.

Salt Cod Custards with Brioche Toast Fingers and White Truffle Oil

This is meant as a small pre-appetizer course for an elegant dinner party. For a more substantial serving you could surround the ramekin with lightly dressed tender greens.

---

1 lb thick bone-in dried salt cod (excess salt brushed off), chopped in small pieces
2 cups milk
1 bay leaf
1 small onion, thinly sliced
1 cup half-and-half cream
2 eggs

2 egg yolks
1 tbsp roasted garlic puree (page 94), passed through a sieve
¼ tsp freshly ground white pepper
6 drops hot red pepper sauce
1½ tsp white truffle oil (page 112)
Sliced brioche or challah, crusts removed

Cover cod with water, cover and refrigerate for 12 to 24 hours. Change water four times during soaking.

Drain cod and place in large saucepan. Barely cover with milk and bring to boil. Cover and simmer slowly for 1 hour. Add bay leaf and onion and simmer for 15 minutes more.

Preheat oven to 300°F.

Strain cod liquid into measuring cup. (Strained liquid should resemble skim milk.) Save cod for another use.

Add enough cream to bring liquid back up to 2 cups. Taste. If mixture is too salty, add a bit more cream.

Whisk together eggs and egg yolks in large bowl for about 30 seconds. Add garlic. Gradually whisk 2 cups milk mixture into eggs. Season with white pepper and hot pepper sauce.

Divide mixture evenly among 10 small ramekins. Place ramekins in large baking dish and fill with boiling water to come halfway up sides of ramekins.

Bake for 40 minutes. Custards should be set yet slightly "jiggly."

Place ramekins on serving plates. Drizzle a few drops of truffle oil on each custard.

Toast brioche lightly and cut into fingers or points. Place a few pieces of brioche on each plate.

Makes 10 servings.

THE BOSTON TAVERN [MICHAEL CARLEVALE]

HOMEMADE CROUTONS

Cut egg bread into ½-inch cubes. Place on oiled baking sheet and bake at 250°F for 20 minutes, turning once during baking time.

Maybe Toronto wasn't ready for the original incarnation of the Boston Club. Restaurateur Michael Carlevale gave it his all: a glossy, candlelit room, beautiful furniture and a long, dimly lit oyster bar that was one of the great undiscovered cocktail spots in the city. When putting together the menu, he drew on the expertise of legendary New England food guru, Jasper White, whose influence was reflected in the fish and seafood dishes that took up eighty percent of the card: scrod with a crust of cracker crumbs, smoked Boston bluefish with steamed brown bread, steamer clams and these irresistible stuffed quahogs. Canadian chef Scott Saunderson timed his fish to perfection and garnished it exquisitely, but Toronto, more used to shrimp and good old salmon, never quite saw the point of such sophistication. So a few subtle changes were made and the Boston Club became the Boston Tavern. The good news is the place is still a delight.

WINE SUGGESTIONS
Ontario Auxerrois or Aligoté 🍁
Sancerre (Loire)
A dry, fresh white with a name as difficult to pronounce as quahogs.

Baked Stuffed Clams

cherrystone clams

Baked stuffed clams are a Boston tradition. They are usually served on a bed of rock salt (the salt holds the shells steady).

4 oz bacon, diced
4 stalks celery, finely chopped
2 onions, chopped
2 bay leaves
2 cloves garlic, finely chopped
1 cup fish stock or chicken stock
1 cup dry white wine

½ cup vermouth
8 sprigs fresh thyme or ½ tsp dried
4 lb cherrystone clams, cleaned
5 cups croutons
¼ cup chopped fresh parsley
3 tbsp chopped fresh oregano or 2 tsp dried
Salt and freshly ground pepper to taste

Preheat oven to 350°F.

Cook bacon in large skillet on medium-high heat until crisp. Remove from pan with slotted spoon, leaving about 2 tbsp bacon fat in skillet.

Add celery and onions to pan and cook, stirring occasionally until softened, about 3 minutes. Stir in bay leaves and garlic and cook for 1 minute. Remove from heat. Stir in bacon.

Combine stock, wine, vermouth and thyme in large saucepan. Bring to boil. Add clams, cover and cook for about 8 minutes or until clams open. Drain, reserving liquid.

Remove clams from shells, reserving shells. Chop clams and add to reserved vegetables along with croutons. Stir in enough reserved liquid to bind mixture. Add parsley, oregano, salt and pepper.

Spoon clam mixture into washed clam shells. Place on baking sheet and bake for 15 to 20 minutes or until golden.

Makes 4 servings.

CENTRO GRILL AND WINE BAR [Marc Thuet]

Marc Thuet does nothing by halves. He is passionate and possessed of superhuman energy, the limits of which he frequently explores. Not content with cooking nightly for the multitudes who flock to Centro, the famous Toronto restaurant he co-owns with front-of-house maestro, Tony Longo, he has developed a highly successful retail line of sauces, dressings and marinades, and has recently bought and renovated a farm where he intends to breed prize Black Angus cattle. But it is his prowess in the kitchen that has won him international acclaim. At its heart lies the rich classicism of his native Alsace, polished and modified by his training under Nouvelle Cuisine pioneer Anton Mosimann at the Dorchester in London, England, and enhanced by his enthusiasm for prime Canadian ingredients. Centro has its own energy, its own glamour, but it is Thuet's personal aesthetic, expanded to embrace the improbable numbers the restaurant serves, that gives substance to the pizzazz.

MANDOLIN

A mandolin is a French slicer that allows you to cut or julienne vegetables very thinly. Inexpensive Japanese versions are available. If you do not have one, try to grate long shreds on the largest holes of a box grater.

WINE SUGGESTIONS
Canadian barrel-fermented Chardonnay 🍁
Napa Chardonnay or Oregon Pinot Gris
A rich, fatty fish needs a white wine with lots of power (or you could go with a red Burgundy and defy convention!).

Atlantic Salmon Tataki with Sesame Cucumber Noodles

This is a beautifully presented dish. The assertive cucumber mixture adds real zing to the full-flavoured salmon.

2 English cucumbers, peeled and seeded
1 tsp salt
1 lb Atlantic salmon fillet, skin removed
Salt and freshly ground pepper to taste
Pinch granulated sugar
3 tbsp sesame oil
2 tbsp lime juice

2 tsp grated lime rind
2 tbsp soy sauce
1 tbsp toasted sesame seeds
1 green onion, chopped
1 red chili pepper, seeded and
   finely diced (optional)
Fresh coriander leaves

Slice cucumber lengthwise into spaghetti-like strips using mandolin. Place in colander and sprinkle with salt. Let stand for 1 hour. Rinse, drain and pat dry.

Season salmon with salt, pepper and sugar. Let stand for 1 hour. Brush with a little of the sesame oil.

Heat heavy non-stick skillet on high heat. Sear salmon for about 1 minute per side. Cool and slice thinly against the grain.

Combine remaining sesame oil, lime juice, lime rind, soy sauce and sesame seeds in large bowl. Add cucumber and toss.

Twist cucumber "spaghetti" around a fork and place on serving plates. Garnish with green onion, chili and coriander and top with salmon slices.

Makes 4 servings.

ESCABÈCHE

[Lee Parsons]

CORIANDER CREAM

Blanch 1 cup fresh coriander leaves in boiling water for 30 seconds. Drain immediately and refresh under cold running water. Squeeze out as much moisture as possible. Puree coriander and ¼ cup milk in food processor. Add ½ cup sour cream and salt, cayenne and sugar to taste. Rub mixture through sieve to create a smooth consistency. Stir in 1 tbsp lime juice just before serving.

Makes about 1 cup.

The Prince of Wales Hotel has been a beloved Niagara-on-the-Lake landmark for 135 years, but it never looked as grand as it did last July, reopened after six months of major renovations by owner Si Wai Lai and her team. One innovation was the creation of Escabèche, an intimate restaurant with a single, simple ambition: to be the best dining room in Canada. With this in mind, Si Wai brought in a new executive chef from England. Lee Parsons spent the first eight years of his career at Claridge's Hotel in London, starting out as an apprentice and rising quickly through the hierarchy to the rank of junior sous-chef. From there he moved to Raymond Blanc's world-famous restaurant, Le Manoir aux Quat' Saisons, as head chef. And thence hither. Still in his twenties, Parsons has learned the sophistication of simplicity. "I want the food to taste of what it is," he says. "The flavours on the plate ought to complement and refine the taste of the principal item." It's a notion that shines in this recipe—appropriately enough, an escabèche.

WINE SUGGESTIONS
Ontario dry Riesling ❦
Muscadet (Loire) or Verdicchio (Marche)
The crisper the wine the better. This dish needs a wine with lively acidity and no oak.

Escabèche of Sea Scallops with Coriander Cream

An escabèche is a marinated fish dish similar to seviche but with the fish cooked either before or after marinating. This lovely summer dish is easy to make, although it has a long list of ingredients. Mache is a sturdy field lettuce that will not wilt in the marinade. Watercress could be substituted.

½ cup orange juice
3 tbsp lime juice
1 heaping tbsp finely chopped pickled ginger
⅓ cup olive oil
18 scallops, cut in half horizontally
2 tbsp olive oil
1 cup peeled and diced eggplant
1 tbsp sherry vinegar

VEGETABLE SALAD:
½ fennel bulb, thinly sliced
1 cup peeled and thinly sliced carrots
⅓ cup thinly sliced celery (strings removed)
1 shallot, thinly sliced

2 plum tomatoes, peeled, seeded and
   each cut into 8 wedges
2 radishes, thinly sliced
1 small green or yellow zucchini, thinly sliced
2 tbsp shredded fresh coriander
2 tbsp shredded fresh basil
1 tbsp chopped fresh parsley
½ cup shredded mache
1½ tsp toasted fennel seeds
1½ tsp hot red chili flakes
1½ tsp finely chopped garlic
Salt and sugar to taste

2 to 4 tsp olive oil

Combine orange juice, lime juice, pickled ginger and ⅓ cup olive oil in small bowl.

Place scallops in large bowl and cover with half the marinade. Cover and refrigerate for 4 to 6 hours.

Heat 2 tbsp olive oil in small skillet over medium-high heat. Carefully add eggplant and vinegar (it will splatter). Reduce heat to medium and cook until soft, about 5 minutes.

Combine eggplant with all remaining vegetable salad ingredients, herbs, seasonings and remaining marinade in large bowl.

Drain scallops from marinade. Heat 2 tsp olive oil in skillet over high heat. In batches, sear scallops on each side until a deep golden colour, about 1 minute. Add more oil if necessary.

Place scallops on 6 serving plates and cover with vegetables. Streak coriander cream (page 46) over plate.

Makes 6 servings.

FAR NIENTE

[HUGH KERR]

When Scottish-born chef Hugh Kerr left Britain in 1983, he must have thought he'd landed in heaven. As chef of a spiffy golf club in Bermuda, he could cycle to work in his swimming trunks every day and head out with his clubs three times a week. No wonder he stayed in the islands for seven years before moving on to Toronto. Here he found work with Gary Hoyer at Amsterdam, becoming chef when Hoyer left a year later. In the fullness of time, Amsterdam was sold and turned into Al Frisco's. Kerr stayed on as chef until 1997, when the company opened Far Niente on Bay Street. A Californian-style restaurant with a renowned wine list of ten thousand bottles, Far Niente is famous for its steaks and salmon, but Kerr decided to prepare a vegetarian dish for Taste '99, taking advantage of the asparagus season and Cookstown Greens' beautiful edible flowers.

WINE SUGGESTIONS
Ontario Sauvignon Blanc ❦
New Zealand Sauvignon Blanc
When there's asparagus in the dish, call for Sauvignon Blanc.

Baby Green and White Asparagus with Marigold Relish and Savoury Tuiles

This recipe calls for fragrant marigold flowers but you could also substitute peppery nasturtium or basil flowers (make sure the flowers have not been sprayed), or you could omit the flowers altogether.

SAVOURY TUILES:
2 egg whites
½ cup icing sugar
⅓ cup all-purpose flour
2 tsp finely chopped fresh rosemary
½ tsp grated lemon rind

MARIGOLD RELISH:
1 tbsp olive oil
1 sweet red pepper, chopped
1 onion, chopped

1 tsp grated orange rind
½ cup orange juice
1 tbsp lemon juice
2 tbsp marigold petals
1 tbsp chopped fresh tarragon
Salt and freshly ground pepper to taste

1 bunch white asparagus, trimmed
1 bunch green asparagus, trimmed
6 cups mixed baby greens

Preheat oven to 400°F. Butter and flour 2 large baking sheets.

Whisk egg whites in bowl until frothy. Sift in icing sugar and flour. Whisk in rosemary and lemon rind until blended. Spoon batter onto baking sheets by the teaspoon, spreading thinly to make 3-inch circles.

Bake for 3 to 5 minutes until edges begin to brown. Let cool slightly. Remove warm tuiles one at a time and gently form each into a cone. (If tuiles cool and become inflexible, return baking sheet to oven to warm and soften.) Let cool completely.

Heat oil over medium-low heat in large skillet. Add red pepper and onion and cook for 10 minutes until softened. Stir in orange rind, orange juice, lemon juice, marigold petals and tarragon. Cook for 5 minutes or until liquid has evaporated. Season with salt and pepper.

Peel asparagus and cut into 1-inch lengths. Blanch in large saucepan of boiling salted water for 2 minutes or until green asparagus is bright green. Drain and refresh under cold running water. Place in large bowl and toss with mixed greens.

Divide asparagus mixture among plates. Top with relish and savoury tuile.

Makes 12 servings.

LA FENICE

[Luigi Orgera]

There was once a restaurant called Latina, on the Queensway, that served wonderful spaghetti vongole. It opened in 1951 and the owner was Luigi Orgera, a young man newly arrived from Italy. Almost half a century later, Orgera is going strong, and so is La Fenice, the place he opened after Latina, back in the early eighties. At the time, it was Toronto's best Italian restaurant; many would say it still is—the room where a whole generation of gourmets first tasted white truffle grated onto pasta and discovered how intricately glorious antipasto could be. Then there is the shrimp, and the risotto, and the way the kitchen grills fish so lightly with just a brush of olive oil from Orgera's own trees—and the artichokes, done in the Roman way.

ARTICHOKES

Artichokes are not as popular in North America as they are in Europe. The problem is the preparation. All the tough outer leaves must be removed and any tender leaves left should have their tips cut off if they are spiky. To prevent the artichokes from turning brown, rub them with hands covered in lemon juice.

WINE SUGGESTIONS
Ontario Sauvignon Blanc ❦
Sancerre (Loire)
Artichokes are one of the most difficult vegetables to match with wine, but the vegetal notes in Sauvignon Blanc from cool climate regions work well.

RACK OF LAMB WITH PECAN HONEY MUSTARD CRUST AND GREEN ONION MINT PESTO (PAGE 107)

LEMON AND ASPARAGUS RISOTTO (PAGE 71)

Artichokes alla Romana
artichokes

Stuffed artichokes are a quintessential Roman dish. Use large artichokes but be sure to remove the tough outer leaves and spiky tips.

1 cup fresh breadcrumbs
⅓ cup olive oil
2 cloves garlic
6 leaves fresh mint

1 tbsp chopped fresh dill
Salt to taste
4 fresh artichokes

Preheat oven to 350°F.

Combine breadcrumbs, 3 tbsp olive oil, garlic, mint, dill and salt in food processor. Process until minced.

Cut stems off artichokes, making bottoms flat. Cut one-third off tops of artichokes. Bang artichokes on work surface to loosen centres.

Discard outer leaves until only pale leaves around base remain. Gently separate centres and pull out chokes with fingers.

Fill centre of each artichoke with herb stuffing. Sprinkle with remaining 2 tbsp olive oil. Place in baking dish and add enough water to come halfway up sides of artichokes. Cover and bake for 45 to 60 minutes or until stuffing is cooked and artichokes are tender.

Makes 4 servings.

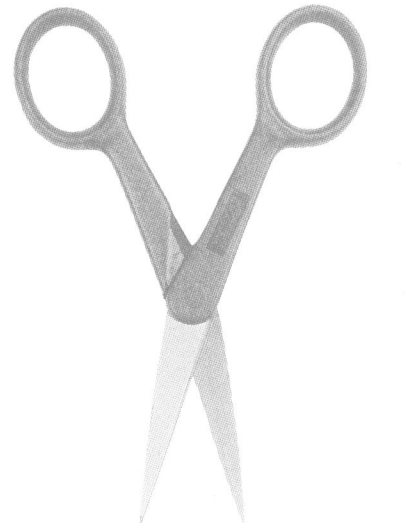

HUMMINGBIRD CENTRE
FOR THE PERFORMING ARTS [KEN PEACE]

SAFFRON

Saffron is the most expensive spice in the world. It is gathered from the stamens of crocuses in the Mediterranean. Always buy it in threads or strands, which have much more taste than the powder. Dissolving it in a little warm water before using will bring out the flavour.

Ken Peace never meant to be a chef. In his youth, he set out from Toronto to seek his fortune in the Alberta oil fields but ended up taking a temporary job as a kitchen porter at Chateau Lake Louise. "After two weeks of that, I entered the hotel's apprentice program," he recalls, "and I've been stuck in a kitchen ever since, first in Alberta, then B.C. and then Queensland, Australia, before coming back to Toronto in 1984." Four years later, he moved into the O'Keefe Centre as executive chef and there he has remained, also serving the industry as president of the Escoffier Society and several other prestigious organizations. A decade ago, Ken helped pioneer the idea of using a gathering of chefs to raise money for charity, and he has been a keen participant of every Taste ever since. This salmon recipe, with its delicately tart lime crust, is based on the techniques he developed while cooking in the South Pacific.

WINE SUGGESTIONS
Ontario Auxerrois ✳
Muscadet or very dry sparkling wine
A fresh, lively white wine, unoaked, is best for this dish, but to make it very special choose a very dry sparkling wine (such as Brut champagne).

Salmon Skewers in Lime Pepper Crust with Caviar and Herbed Yogurt

caviar and herbed yogurt

This spicy salmon dish can be also be served as a main course with steamed jasmine rice and stir-fried watercress and mushrooms. Red lumpfish caviar can be substituted for the salmon caviar.

HERBED YOGURT:
1 tsp saffron threads
2 tsp warm water
¾ cup yogurt
¼ cup sour cream
¼ cup salmon caviar
1 tbsp finely chopped fresh basil
1 tbsp finely chopped fresh chives
1 tbsp finely chopped fresh coriander
1 tbsp finely chopped fresh dill
Salt and freshly ground pepper to taste

SALMON SKEWERS:
Juice and grated rind of 3 limes
3 tbsp finely chopped shallots
1 tbsp mustard powder
Salt to taste
1 lb salmon fillet, skinned
2 tbsp cracked black peppercorns

Soak saffron in warm water for 30 minutes.

Stir together saffron mixture with yogurt, sour cream, caviar, basil, chives, coriander and dill in small bowl. Season with salt and pepper. Cover and refrigerate for at least 1 hour, or overnight.

Soak six 6-inch wooden skewers in water for 30 minutes.

Whisk together lime juice, shallots, mustard powder and salt in small bowl.

Cut salmon into 24 1-inch cubes. Put 4 cubes on each skewer and place in shallow dish. Pour lime mixture over and marinate for 30 minutes.

Combine lime rind and cracked pepper on plate. Roll salmon skewers in pepper mixture. Brush salmon lightly with oil and grill on medium-high heat for about 2 minutes, turning to cook all sides, until barely cooked at centre.

Spoon yogurt sauce on each plate and top with skewer.

Makes 6 servings.

JOSO'S

[JOSO AND LEO SPRALJA]

CLEANING SQUID

To clean squid, pull tentacles and innards from body. Cut off tentacles just above the eyes; discard eyes and innards. Pull transparent piece of cartilage from squid sac and discard. Peel purple skin away from sac under running water and discard. Cut sac crosswise into ½-inch strips to form rings.

All the way down the coast of Dalmatia and Italy's Adriatic, the lucky traveller comes across treasures—small, casual, surprisingly expensive restaurants that specialize in fresh fish and shellfish, squid and cuttlefish and maybe risotto made with cuttlefish ink. Joso's brings such delights to Toronto. In that tight, bright little two-storey house full of noisy locals and visiting movie stars, watched over by founder Joso Spralja's artwork (best described, perhaps, as reflections on a marine Venus), the raw fish is brought to the table for customers' inspection. By the time it returns, chef Leo Spralja has cooked it, very simply and well, with a little oil, a pinch of salt, some parsley and lemon juice and a few careful minutes on the grill. The only thing as sure as this kitchen's touch with fish is its way with octopus, cuttlefish… and calamari.

WINE SUGGESTIONS
Ontario dry Riesling or BC Pinot Blanc ❋
Chablis (Burgundy) or Muscadet (Loire)
Fried seafood calls for a very dry white wine to cleanse the palate of oil and salt.

Calamari Fritti calamari

The crispiest squid ever. Serve in a basket with lemon wedges.

---

4 medium squid (about 1¼ lb),
    cleaned with tentacles
Vegetable oil for deep frying

1 cup all-purpose flour
Salt to taste
Lemon wedges

Cut squid into ½-inch rings.

Place 2 inches vegetable oil in deep-fryer, wok or deep, heavy saucepan. Heat to 375°F (or until a cube of bread turns brown in 15 seconds).

Mix squid with flour in batches, shaking through sieve to remove excess flour. Fry for 3 minutes or until golden and crisp. Drain on paper towels. Sprinkle with salt and garnish with lemon wedges.

Makes 4 servings.

JOV BISTRO

[OWEN STEINBERG]

RED WINE VINAIGRETTE

Whisk together 1 tbsp dry red wine, 2 tsp red wine vinegar, ¼ tsp Dijon mustard, ¼ cup olive oil and salt and freshly ground pepper to taste.

Makes about ⅓ cup.

It wasn't long ago that all Leaside was abuzz with the news of JOV's arrival in the neighbourhood, a new bistro with an intriguing menu and the most wonderful cooking. Three years later, it's still hard to get a table. The name is an acronym of the restaurant's three youthful owners—chef Owen Steinberg, his twin sister Jill and their friend Virginie Gysel, both of whom work the front of the house. Owen had been sous-chef at Azalea under Didier Leroy, and there is a classical precision beneath the imaginative conception of his dishes that has already made him one of the city's brightest rising stars.

CURRY CREAM

Stir 1 tsp curry powder in small skillet on medium-high heat until fragrant. Reduce heat to medium and add 1 cup whipping cream. Cook until reduced by half or until sauce coats back of spoon, about 10 to 15 minutes. Season with salt and freshly ground pepper to taste.

WINE SUGGESTIONS
Canadian Sauvignon Blanc 🍁
Sancerre (Loire)
A whole lot of taste sensations to contend with here; go with a crisp Sauvignon Blanc.

Scallop Boudin

These scallop sausages must be handled gently to prevent them from bursting. However, if they do burst, just remove from casings and slice. You could also simply roll the scallop mixture into three sausages using plastic wrap to encase them. Tie the ends with twist ties and cook in simmering water for 20 minutes or until firm. Cool, unwrap, cut into slices and cook briefly in a little olive oil in a non-stick pan.

The carrot and cucumber strings are usually cut with a mandolin (page 44), but you can also shred them in a food processor.

BOUDIN:
1 lb scallops
1 egg white
1 cup whipping cream
Salt and freshly ground pepper to taste
¼ cup chopped fresh chives
3 feet sausage casings

ARUGULA SALAD:
1 bunch arugula, trimmed
1½ cups carrot strings
1½ cups cucumber strings
1 tbsp chopped fresh coriander
3 tbsp chopped green onions
1 tbsp finely chopped shallot
¼ cup red wine vinaigrette (page 56)

Chop scallops in food processor until chunky. Add egg white, whipping cream, salt and pepper and puree. Stir in chives.

Fill pastry bag (fitted with plain tip) with mixture and stuff casings (or use plastic wrap as described above). Tie off ends at 5-inch intervals and separate to make six sausages.

Place sausages in large saucepan of cold water and bring just to light simmer. Cook very gently until solid to touch, 10 to 12 minutes. Drain.

Toss arugula, carrot, cucumber, coriander, green onions and shallot in large bowl.

Cook sausages gently in non-stick skillet on low heat until golden and heated through.

Toss salad with vinaigrette. Divide salad among 6 plates, place boudin on top and drizzle with curry cream (page 56).

Makes 6 servings.

KRISTAPSONS

[ANDRIS GRINBERGS]

SMOKED SALMON

Smoked salmon varies from country to country. Scottish salmon, for example, is more heavily smoked than Canadian salmon. Today the herbs and spices used in smoking can create a wide range of flavours, from pastrami to Asian spiced.

Forty-nine years ago, on a quiet stretch of Queen Street East, Latvian-born Adolph Kristapson opened a small but well-stocked European-style deli. The business did okay, but it was the salmon he smoked in the rear of the premises that kept customers coming back. When Osvalds Indzers bought the business in 1964, he carried on smoking fish in the moist, slightly sweet, lightly cured Latvian style, and gradually everything else in the store disappeared. Indzers' nephew, Andris Grinbergs, took over the store in 1988 and saw no reason to change a thing. Smoked, farmed coho is still the only product he sells, at the Queen Street address and at the tiny cadet branch on Yonge Street north of Lawrence Avenue. The fish is cured and smoked to order because Grinbergs insists it be fresh, never frozen, though there's usually a pound or two available for customers who forget to call ahead. Grinbergs keeps an eye open for terrific smoked salmon recipes to serve at the many charity events with which he is involved. This recipe is based on one given to him by Seka Sefter.

WINE SUGGESTIONS
Canadian dry Riesling or Gewürztraminer 🍁
Alsace Gewürztraminer
Smoked salmon and Gewürztraminer is a great combination. If you can't find Gewürz, go for a dry Riesling.

Smoked Salmon Cheesecake
smoked salmon

Serve this magnificent cheesecake with a salad as a first course or on top of rye bread as an hors d'oeuvre. It is also a lovely brunch dish.

1¼ lb soft deli-style cream cheese
12 oz ricotta cheese
4 eggs, lightly beaten
⅓ cup whipping cream
1 tbsp all-purpose flour
Salt and freshly ground pepper to taste
8 oz smoked salmon, coarsely chopped

¼ cup finely chopped fresh chives
2 tbsp finely chopped fresh dill or 2 tsp dried
1½ cups sour cream
8 oz smoked salmon, thinly sliced
Sliced English cucumber
Fresh dill sprigs

Preheat oven to 325°F. Line bottom of 8-inch springform pan with circle of parchment paper. Place pan on large square of heavy-duty foil and press foil up around all sides of pan to prevent water from soaking into cake.

Beat cream cheese and ricotta with electric mixer until smooth. Add eggs, whipping cream, flour, salt and pepper. Stir in chopped smoked salmon, chives and dill. Pour mixture into prepared pan.

Set springform pan in larger pan and pour hot water around springform to come 1 inch up sides. Bake for 1½ hours.

Remove from oven and reduce heat to 300°F. Spread sour cream evenly over top of cheesecake. Return to oven for 5 minutes. Remove from larger pan, remove foil, and cool on rack to room temperature. Cover with plastic wrap and refrigerate until completely chilled and set.

Transfer cheesecake to serving plate and top with sliced smoked salmon. Garnish with sliced cucumber and sprigs of dill.

Makes 16 to 20 servings.

LANGDON HALL [JAMES SAUNDERS]

I remember the first time I tasted James Saunders' cooking. He had just arrived from Horsted Place, a grand country house hotel in England, to take on the duties of executive chef at the Sherwood Inn in Muskoka. Every dish he presented was marked by a simple, elegant, self-disciplined grace that flattered his carefully sourced ingredients. It was English country house cooking at its best, and it turned Sherwood Inn into a gourmets' destination for all the years he was there. Now, after a period at The Waterside Inn in Port Credit, Saunders has taken over Louise Duhamel's kitchen at Langdon Hall, and it reads like a perfect fit. As created by owners Bill Bennett and Mary Beaton, Langdon Hall is as stately a home as Ontario can offer, discreetly concealing a state-of-the-art spa and other very contemporary luxuries to delight its guests. And Saunders will have the bounty of gardener Matthew Smerek's justifiably famous vegetable garden, greenhouses and orchards with which to play. I hope he remembers to bring his awesome recipe for smoking salmon with him.

WINE SUGGESTIONS
Canadian Sauvignon Blanc 🍁
Pouilly-Fumé or Sancerre (Loire Valley)
When it comes to goat cheese the best marriage is with a youthful Sauvignon Blanc.

Ontario Goat Cheese Mousseline with Eggplant Confit

You can spread the goat cheese on toast rounds and serve with a salad, if desired. The eggplant confit also makes an interesting accompaniment with rack of lamb.

½ cup olive oil
2 Italian eggplants, sliced in very thin rounds
2 sprigs fresh thyme or pinch dried
1 sprig fresh rosemary or pinch dried
2 bay leaves
Salt and freshly ground pepper to taste
1 tsp honey
2 cloves garlic, peeled
2 tbsp red wine vinegar

2 tbsp balsamic vinegar
2 tbsp sherry vinegar
1 tomato, seeded and thinly sliced
1 small onion, thinly sliced
½ cup goat cheese
1 tbsp whipping cream
1 tsp chopped fresh parsley
1 tsp chopped fresh thyme or ¼ tsp dried
Freshly ground pepper to taste

Heat oil in large skillet on medium heat. Add eggplant and cook for 5 minutes, turning once, until browned.

Add thyme and rosemary sprigs, bay leaves, salt, pepper, honey, garlic and vinegars to skillet and simmer gently over low heat for 15 minutes, shaking pan occasionally. Remove from heat and stir in tomato and onion. Let cool, cover and refrigerate for 2 days.

Place goat cheese in bowl and combine with cream, parsley, chopped thyme and pepper.

Arrange four slices of eggplant slightly overlapping on each plate.

Mould goat cheese into oval-shaped quenelles with 2 dessert spoons heated in hot water. Place on eggplant. Spoon marinade over top.

Makes 4 to 6 servings.

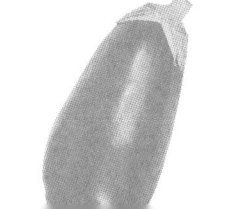

PANGAEA

"Think globally but use local ingredients." That is one of the mottos that informs Martin Kouprie's menus at Pangaea—menus that ring with thoughtful, classic methods and techniques transformed by a clean, light, modern touch and flavours that seduce the palate instead of trying to bamboozle it. Pronto was his first kitchen, then Jump, and now Pangaea, the restaurant he created with partner Peter Geary in the historic space once occupied by Noodles and Acrobat. The place is always busy—packed at lunchtime and dinner, with the gap between bridged by a formal, pleasingly traditional service of afternoon tea.

WINE SUGGESTIONS
Canadian Chardonnay 🍁
Gavi (Piedmont) or Valpolicella (Veneto)
Best go for Italian for this creamy polenta with cheese and nut highlights.
White wine lovers should try the Gavi; for red, Valpolicella.

POLENTA

Polenta is an Italian coarse-grained yellow cornmeal cooked with liquid. It can be soft and creamy or very firm, depending on the amount of liquid you use. Firm polenta can be grilled and served with various toppings.

Polenta should be cooked and stirred for about 15 minutes to achieve the right consistency, but instant polenta is also available.

Silken Green Pumpkin Seed Polenta

This cheesy, pungent, nutty polenta is soft and creamy. It can be eaten alone or served with roasted or braised lamb, pork or chicken. Pumpkin seeds are available at specialty food stores. They are sometimes called pepitas.

1 tbsp vegetable oil
1 onion, finely diced
2½ cups milk
1 clove garlic, finely chopped
Dash hot red pepper sauce
½ cup cornmeal

⅓ cup toasted green pumpkin seeds
⅓ cup grated Parmesan cheese
1 tbsp chopped fresh parsley
Salt and freshly ground pepper to taste
Pinch grated nutmeg

Heat oil in large, heavy saucepan over medium-low heat. Cook onion, stirring often, for 8 minutes or until translucent.

Stir in milk, garlic and hot pepper sauce and bring to boil. Reduce heat to low.

Add cornmeal in three additions, stirring in each until fully incorporated. Cook, stirring, for 15 minutes or until polenta is thick and slight crust forms on bottom of saucepan. Stir in pumpkin seeds, Parmesan, parsley, salt, pepper and nutmeg.

Makes 4 servings.

PIATTO

[FREDDY LO CICERO]

Sandro Julita loves mushrooms. Wild mushrooms. He knows where to find them, how to pick them and how to prepare them the way the angels do. So if you should go to his eleven-year-old Mississauga restaurant, Piatto, and there's something with mushrooms on the menu or on the huge blackboard of specials (and there always is), order it. Not that Sandro cooks at Piatto. This recipe evolved in the hands of chef Freddy Lo Cicero who joined Piatto in 1999. He, too, is a funghi aficionado. No one makes mushroom soup like Freddy—or calves' liver, or chopped wild mushrooms in soft brioche with white truffle whipped cream. Mushrooms again? Thank goodness.

WINE SUGGESTIONS
Canadian oak-aged Chardonnay ☙
Chilean Chardonnay or Oregon Pinot Noir
The creamy mousse suggests an oak-aged white with good fruit or, for the less conventional choice, a Pinot Noir with good fruit and lively acidity.

Mediterranean Fish Terrine with Morels

This sophisticated terrine is very rich, so serve small pieces with a slice of baguette and a garnish of watercress. If morels are unavailable, use shiitake mushrooms.

⅓ cup whipping cream
2 slices white bread, crusts removed
2 tsp butter
⅓ cup sliced onions
Salt and freshly ground pepper to taste
Pinch cayenne
8 oz skinless, boneless salmon fillet, sliced

1 egg white
Pinch grated nutmeg
1 cup whipping cream, cold
5 morels, well washed
1¼ lb skinless, boneless cod, snapper
   or sea bass
4 cups fish stock or water

Pour ⅓ cup whipping cream over bread in bowl. Let sit until all cream is absorbed, about 10 minutes.

Heat 1 tsp butter in small skillet over medium-high heat. Add onions and cook for 5 minutes or until softened. Stir in salt, pepper and cayenne. Transfer to bowl, cover and cool.

Combine salmon, egg white, nutmeg and soaked bread in food processor until smooth. Push mixture through sieve into bowl to produce very smooth texture. Place bowl filled with salmon mixture in larger bowl filled with ice to keep mixture cold and help set mousse.

Whip 1 cup cold whipping cream in bowl until it holds its shape. Fold gently into salmon mixture. Refrigerate.

Heat remaining 1 tsp butter in skillet over medium heat. Add morels and cook for 5 minutes or until softened. Cool slightly and slice into thin strips. Slice cod into long thin strips. Season with salt and pepper.

Place half of mousse on large piece of oiled heavy-duty foil. Lay cod and morels lengthwise on top of mousse. Top with remaining mousse. Twist ends of foil and roll up gently to form log 1½ inches in diameter.

Poach foil log in saucepan of simmering fish stock for 15 to 20 minutes. Cool. Unmould and slice. (You can also layer mousse, cod and mushrooms in terrine or loaf pan. Cover with foil and place in roasting pan. Pour boiling water into roasting pan to come halfway up sides of terrine dish. Bake in preheated 350°F oven for 30 minutes. Remove from oven and cool in pan.)

Makes 10 to 12 servings.

ROYAL YORK HOTEL [JOHN K. CORDEAUX]

PEA SHOOTS

Pea shoots are the top leaves and tendrils of the snow pea vine. They add crunch and a spring-like taste to salads and stir-fries.

Englishman John K. Cordeaux simply exudes cheerful energy. He needed it when he was simultaneously executive chef of the Queen Elizabeth Hotel in Montreal and of the Molson Centre, with its endless array of private boxes and two restaurants. He still needs it as executive chef of the Royal York, with all the thousands of meals and banquets prepared in those gargantuan kitchens. He had barely arrived in Toronto when the chance came to contribute to Taste '99. "In Quebec," he explains, "I always used Allegheny trout so I asked around, trying to find a local equivalent that was as good. Then I tried these hot-smoked Manitoulin trout and they were gorgeous, especially in this combination with the couscous, curry and new potato."

BERRY VINAIGRETTE
Whisk together 2 tbsp cloud berries or raspberries with ¼ cup grapeseed oil, ¼ cup raspberry vinegar, 1 tbsp vegetable oil, 1 tbsp finely chopped shallots and salt and freshly ground pepper to taste. Makes about ⅔ cup.

WINE SUGGESTIONS
BC Pinot Blanc or off-dry Ontario Riesling ✷
Alsace Muscat or German Riesling Spätlese
Smoked fish requires a white wine with good acidity and a touch of residual sugar.

Smoked Manitoulin Trout on a Steamed New Potato

Beet chips, curried yogurt and smoked trout combine to make an exceptional appetizer. If you do not have the cumin and fenugreek, double the amount of curry powder.

---

1 beet, peeled and thinly sliced
Pinch salt
2 lb small new potatoes (about 40)
¼ tsp curry powder
Pinch ground cumin
Pinch ground fenugreek (page 98)
¼ cup yogurt
1 tbsp white vinegar
¼ tsp finely chopped garlic
Salt and freshly ground pepper to taste
1½ cups chicken stock
½ tsp saffron threads or tumeric

1 cup couscous
¼ cup grilled corn kernels
2 tbsp chopped fresh parsley
2 tbsp chopped fresh coriander
2 tbsp olive oil
2 tbsp finely chopped red onion
1 tbsp cracked black peppercorns
12 oz smoked Manitoulin Island trout
    or other smoked trout

⅔ cup berry vinaigrette (page 66)
1 cup pea shoots or watercress

Preheat oven to 425°F. Place beet slices on parchment paper-lined baking sheet and bake for 20 minutes or until crisp. Turn once during baking. Break beet chips into pieces and sprinkle with salt.

Steam or boil potatoes until tender; drain and cool. Cut thin slice from and top of each potato. Scoop out middle of potatoes, reserving flesh for another use.

Combine curry powder, cumin, fenugreek, yogurt, vinegar, garlic, salt and pepper in small bowl.

Bring chicken stock to boil in saucepan; add saffron. Stir in couscous. Remove from heat, cover and let stand for 5 minutes or until liquid is absorbed. Fluff couscous with fork. Stir in corn, parsley, coriander, olive oil, onion and cracked pepper.

Cut smoked trout into 1-inch pieces.

Toss pea shoots with half the vinaigrette.

Fill potatoes with couscous. Top with beet chip, then trout. Place pea shoots on top. Drizzle with yogurt cream and remaining vinaigrette.

Makes 12 servings.

LA SCALA

[J. Charles Grieco]

In its heyday, they say, more of Premier Bill Davis's Tory party cabinet meetings took place in La Scala's discreet private dining rooms than at Queen's Park. From the moment John Grieco and his son, Charles, opened their restaurant in the handsome old building on Bay Street, they knew they had a success on their hands. Most of the highly professional staff came from the recently closed Lord Simcoe Hotel; so did the dazzling array of silverware, all monogrammed LS. The menu offered the obligatory steak and lobster but surrounded by a sophisticated northern Italian menu that consciously, and most unusually for the 1960s, avoided the clichés of spaghetti and veal parmigiana. Today, politicians claim that they have no time for long, long lunches, but does Queen's Park run any more smoothly than it did in the days of La Scala's reign?

WINE SUGGESTIONS
Ontario Pinot Grigio 🍁
Alto Adige Pinot Grigio or Soave (Italy)
Go Italian with a lively white wine to balance the saltiness of the Parmigiano Reggiano.

Risotto alla Milanese

Serve this savoury, traditional risotto as a side dish with osso buco or on its own as a first course. The marrow from the osso buco bones may be used in the dish if you wish.

Keep the stock at a gentle simmer at all times to keep the risotto cooking evenly. If you do not have homemade stock, use stock made from good-quality concentrate or canned low-salt broth mixed with twice the recommended amount of water.

---

5 cups beef or veal stock
½ tsp crushed saffron threads
¼ cup butter
⅓ cup finely chopped onion
1½ cups Italian Arborio rice

½ cup dry white wine
1 tbsp bone marrow (optional)
Salt and freshly ground pepper to taste
⅓ cup grated Parmigiano Reggiano cheese

Bring stock to boil in saucepan. Reduce heat to maintain simmer. Stir in saffron to dissolve.

Melt 3 tbsp butter in heavy saucepan over medium heat. Cook onion for 2 minutes or until transparent. Add rice; stir for 1 minute or until all grains are coated. Add wine; stir until it is completely absorbed. Stir in bone marrow, if using.

Add ½ cup simmering stock, stirring constantly until stock is nearly absorbed. Continue to cook, adding stock ½ cup at a time and stirring constantly for 18 to 20 minutes, or until rice is tender with slight firmness at centre. Reduce amount of stock added to ¼ cup as you near end of cooking time. (You may not need all of the stock.) Turn off heat.

Stir in remaining 1 tsp butter, salt, pepper and cheese. Serve immediately.

Makes 4 servings.

SCARAMOUCHE

[KEITH FROGGETT]

RISOTTO RICES

There are different types of Italian short-grain rice used for risotto. *Vialone Nano* (the choice for Venetian-style risottos, which are more soupy) and *Arborio* are the best known. *Carnaroli*, the most expensive risotto rice, has a delectable creaminess and good firm texture when cooked.

Keith Froggett cooked in hotels when he first left England and came to Toronto—at Sutton Place and then the Inn on the Park. You couldn't say he was happy. Then he went to work at Fenton's, and suddenly he remembered why he had wanted to become a chef. In 1984 he moved to Scaramouche and has been there ever since, pretty much, becoming an owner ten years later, with front of house dynamo Carl Korte as his partner. Together they have established and sustained Scaramouche as a shining example of stable, consistent quality, suave but familiar, comfortable but still debonair. Adding the Pasta Bar was a brilliant stroke, giving their restaurant a more casual wing that nonetheless shares the same standards of service, the same wine list, the same mesmerizing view of the distant downtown.

WINE SUGGESTIONS
Ontario Sauvignon Blanc ❉
New Zealand Sauvignon Blanc or Sancerre (Loire)
Citrus and vegetal flavours—a description that could fit Sauvignon Blanc.

Lemon and Asparagus Risotto

asparagus

The combination of flavours makes this an excellent first course as well as a good side dish to serve with simple grilled foods.

6 cups chicken stock	12 oz asparagus, trimmed and cut in 2-inch lengths
½ cup butter	¼ cup grated Parmigiano Reggiano cheese
1 Spanish onion, finely diced	¼ cup finely chopped fresh parsley
2 oz pancetta, finely diced	1 tsp grated lemon rind
1¾ cups Italian Carnaroli rice	2 tbsp lemon juice, or to taste

Bring stock to boil in saucepan. Reduce heat to maintain simmer.

Melt ¼ cup butter in large heavy saucepan over medium heat. Cook onion and pancetta for 4 minutes, stirring, until onion is transparent. Add rice. Stir for 3 minutes or until all grains are coated.

Ladle in ½ cup stock, stirring constantly and waiting until stock is completely absorbed before adding next ½ cup. Continue to cook for 15 minutes, adding stock ½ cup at a time and stirring constantly.

Stir in asparagus. Continue to cook, adding stock ¼ cup at a time and stirring constantly, for 5 minutes or until asparagus is tender and rice is tender with slight firmness at centre. (You may not need all of the stock.) Turn off heat.

Stir in remaining ¼ cup butter, cheese, parsley, lemon rind and juice. Serve immediately.

Makes 6 servings.

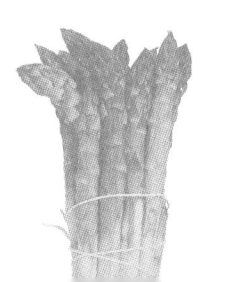
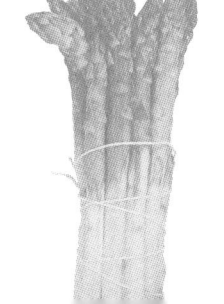

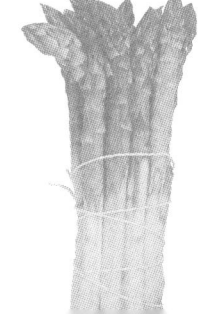

Sen5es

When Henry Wu, owner of the Metropolitan Hotel, decides to do something, he does not do it by halves. Sen5es is just one example. The gourmet food store on the ground floor sells only the most desirable, the most beautiful items. The restaurant above it, with its endlessly interesting view of Bloor Street, aims to be one of the finest in the city. To this end, Wu and his corporate executive chef, Neal Noble, recently brought in Ned Bell as restaurant chef. Coming from Lumière in Vancouver, Bell had made a terrific impression in his first Toronto kitchen, at Accolade in the Crowne Plaza Hotel. Now he has Henry Wu's burgeoning empire behind him—not to mention all the good things on sale in the store below with which to play, creating ever more tantalizing feasts for the senses.

Wine Suggestions
Canadian unoaked Chardonnay 🍁
white Burgundy
Choose a fresh, dry white wine to cleanse the palate of the smoky, fish flavour.

Pan-seared Scallops with Smoked Black Cod and White Bean Puree

The smoked cod mixed with the white beans is similar to a light brandade mixture (page 40). If black cod is not available, use other thick smoked fish such as smoked salmon belly. Use the largest scallops you can find, or buy sixteen smaller scallops and serve two per person.

1 cup dried white kidney beans	2 tbsp white truffle oil (page 112)
¼ cup chopped carrot	¼ cup grapeseed oil
¼ cup chopped celery	Salt and freshly ground pepper to taste
2 cloves garlic, peeled	2 tbsp olive oil
1 sprig fresh thyme	8 oz smoked black cod, cut in 1-inch cubes
1 bay leaf	8 large sea scallops
2 tbsp Champagne vinegar	Fresh chives or chervil sprigs
½ tsp Dijon mustard	

Soak beans overnight in cold water. Drain beans and put in saucepan with carrot, celery, garlic, thyme and bay leaf. Cover with cold water by several inches. Bring to boil, reduce heat to medium and cook for 1 hour or until beans are tender, adding extra water as necessary. Drain and discard bay leaf.

Puree beans and vegetables in food processor until smooth. Press warm mixture through sieve, discarding remaining solids.

Whisk vinegar into mustard in small bowl. Gradually add truffle oil, then grapeseed oil, whisking constantly. Season with salt and pepper.

Heat 1 tbsp olive oil in large skillet over medium-high heat. Cook cod for 1 minute or until heated through. Remove pan from heat. Stir in bean puree, flaking cod as you mix to create a chunky effect. Season with salt and pepper.

Heat remaining 1 tbsp olive oil in separate skillet over medium-high heat. Cook scallops for 4 minutes, turning half-way through cooking time, or until golden on both sides and barely cooked at centre.

Place scallops on plates. Top with cod-bean mixture; drizzle with vinaigrette. Garnish with chives or chervil.

Makes 8 servings.

SOUTHERN ACCENT [ELENA EMBRIONI]

SOUTHERN ACCENT'S
BLACKENING MIX

Sift together ¼ cup paprika,
2 tsp salt, 1 tbsp onion powder,
1 tbsp garlic powder and 2 tsp
cayenne. Stir in 2 tsp freshly
ground white pepper, 2 tsp
freshly ground black pepper,
1 tsp dried thyme, 1 tsp dried
oregano and 1 tsp dried basil.

Makes about ½ cup.

How to describe Southern Accent? As the place for a wicked Bourbon Sour at that dramatically swooping, vintage 1940s bar, sipped to rare-groove Cajun and Zydeco sounds? As the home of the organic farmers' market on Saturday mornings? As the best and indeed only Cajun Creole restaurant in town where customers can finish their meal with a psychic reading by one of the resident fortune tellers. "Lagniappe means 'a little something extra,'" explains owner Frances Wood, and Southern Accent is just dripping with lagniappes. And then there is the cooking—true Louisiana style in the hands of chef Elena Embrioni, but with a thoroughly contemporary emphasis on vegetables. Blackened tempeh is a current hit; blackened chicken livers have been a classic ever since Wood first cranked up the Zydeco fifteen years ago.

WINE SUGGESTIONS
Canadian Merlot ❧
Rhône red (Crozes-Hermitage, Côtes du Rhône)
A gutsy, full-bodied red will stand up to the charred, spicy flavours of this dish.

BEER SUGGESTION
Best bitter
The classic British ale has maltiness to match the richness of the livers, and hops to counter the spice of the blackening.

Blackened Chicken Livers

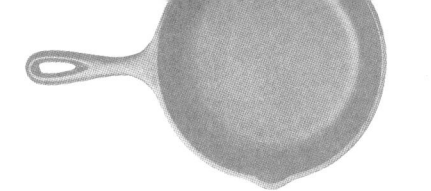

blackened

If you do not have a barbecue you can cook the livers in a cast-iron skillet, but you need a good ventilation system to deal with the smoke. The lemon beurre can also be served with berries.

LEMON BEURRE:
½ cup granulated sugar
Juice of 2 lemons
½ cup butter, cut in 4 pieces
2 cups whipping cream

CHICKEN LIVERS:
3 tbsp blackening mix
2 lb chicken livers, halved
½ cup butter, melted

Combine sugar and lemon juice in heavy saucepan. Bring to boil, reduce heat and simmer until reduced by half, about 10 minutes (syrup should be thick enough to coat spoon).

Stir in butter one piece at a time, allowing each piece to melt completely before adding the next. Slowly stir in whipping cream. Cool for 1 hour.

Place blackening mix in plastic bag. Add livers and toss until well coated. Remove from bag and shake off excess.

Place livers on barbecue preheated to highest heat. Drizzle with half the melted butter (butter will flame up and blacken livers). When flame dies down, turn livers and drizzle with more butter. Cook for 3 minutes in total or until livers are cooked but still pink inside.

Serve with lemon beurre.

Makes 6 to 8 servings.

TRATTORIA GIANCARLO [Eugenia Barato]

Just off the main College Street strip, behind a delightful sidewalk patio, stands Trattoria Giancarlo, a cosy candlelit room that has stood close to the culinary heart of Little Italy for the past sixteen years. Entirely self-taught, chef-owner Eugenia Barato has passed on her skill at the grill and passion for simple, vivid flavours to her son, Jason, who cooked along-side her before his recent promotion to chef de cuisine. This carpaccio is a perennial favourite on the Trattoria's menu and was one of the most popular offerings at Taste '99.

CARPACCIO

Carpaccio is named after a sixteenth-century Venetian painter. The spice used, black pepper, was a commodity originally controlled by the Venetians. It was very expensive and was used as a sign of solvency, making carpaccio a most exclusive dish.

WINE SUGGESTIONS
Ontario Pinot Noir 🍁
Beaujolais or Valpolicella
Choose a light-bodied red wine with good acidity—a young Pinot Noir or a Gamay.

Seared Beef Tenderloin "Carpaccio"

Seared brown on the outside and practically raw inside, this is an exciting version of carpaccio. Serve on a bed of arugula.

---

1 lb beef tenderloin
2 tsp kosher salt
2 tbsp cracked black peppercorns
½ cup olive oil

¼ cup Cognac, warm
¼ cup balsamic vinegar
Shavings of Parmigiano Reggiano
Dash white truffle oil (page 112)

Rub beef with salt and peppercorns.

Heat ¼ cup olive oil in skillet over high heat. Brown meat on all sides, about 1 minute per side.

Add Cognac to skillet and ignite. When flame dissipates, remove from heat. Pour in vinegar and remaining ¼ cup olive oil.

Transfer meat to bowl. Pour over pan juices and cool. Freeze for 15 minutes just before slicing to make slicing easier.

Slice meat very thinly. Arrange on serving platter. Garnish with Parmesan and drizzle with truffle oil.

Makes 6 servings.

TRUFFLES

[PATRICK LIN]

The Four Seasons Hotel threw a tearful farewell party in Truffles' kitchen the day Patrick Lin announced that he was leaving Toronto and heading back to Hong Kong. It was a time for reminiscence. Guests remembered the dazzling menus that Patrick and executive chef Susan Weaver had put together between 1990 and 1994, spanning the million-dollar renovation that turned what looked like a hybrid Franco-Spanish manor house into a sleek, timelessly modern dining room worthy to be the flagship property of a major international hotel chain. But it was the architecture of Lin's plates that inspired real nostalgia, and the wit—a commodity that is rarer than steak tartare in the restaurant industry. Remember a matchless fillet of black bass with scales of tissue-thin potato swimming through lemongrass fronds and a frothy fumet sabayon. Remember a "paper bag" of dark chocolate filled with pineapple milkshake to suck through a chocolate straw.

Patrick left to be executive chef of Quo Quo in Hong Kong, then chef de cuisine at the Excelsior Hotel. And then he came back to Truffles to resume his work, the Asian character of his cooking a little more pronounced, the flawless classical technique, and the wit, as seductive as ever. He did not stay long. These days Patrick is the executive chef of the Metropolitan Hotel and Truffles has reinvented itself yet again, with a young French talent, Thomas Bellac, at the stoves.

WINE SUGGESTIONS
Canadian Chardonnay 🍁
California or Australian Chardonnay
Rich, earthy, salty flavours call for a full-bodied Chardonnay with some oak.

Truffled Nova Scotia Scallops with Asian Mushrooms Salad

A luxe dish that is well worth the expense. Easy to make and rich—a little goes a long way. Use excellent-quality olive oil if you do not have walnut oil.

3 tbsp olive oil
4 large shiitake mushroom caps, sliced
1 package enoki mushrooms, trimmed
    and separated
3 small shallots, finely chopped
1 clove garlic, finely chopped
2 tbsp white truffle oil (page 112)
1 tbsp sherry vinegar

4 tsp walnut oil
Salt and freshly ground pepper to taste
¼ cup whipping cream
8 sea scallops
10 g fresh Perigord truffles, chopped (optional)
1 tbsp butter
2 tbsp chopped fresh chives
1 tbsp chopped fresh tarragon

Heat 2 tbsp olive oil in skillet on medium-high heat. Add shiitake and enoki mushrooms, 2 shallots and garlic. Sauté for about 3 minutes, or until mushrooms are tender and beginning to brown. Keep warm.

Whisk together truffle oil, vinegar, walnut oil, salt and pepper in small bowl.

Whip cream to soft peaks in separate bowl. Whisk in truffle oil vinaigrette.

Dry scallops well. Heat remaining 1 tbsp olive oil in large skillet on high heat. Sear scallops on both sides until golden brown, about 2 minutes per side. Reduce heat to low. Add truffles if using, and remaining shallot and butter, stirring until butter is melted. Remove from heat.

Divide mushroom salad among 4 scallop shells or plates. Top with seared scallops and truffle mixture. Drizzle with vinaigrette; garnish with chives and tarragon.

Makes 4 servings.

VINELAND ESTATES WINERY [Mark Picone]

"My first teachers were my parents," recalls Mark Picone, chef at Vineland Estates Winery in Niagara. This is hardly surprising since food is the family business—his grandparents opened Picone's Food Market in Dundas, Ontario, in 1915. Mark worked there for a while after graduating from the University of Guelph, and then headed off to Europe for five years, cooking in restaurants all over France and Italy. He came back to Canada in 1996 and immediately took over the food operations at Vineland. In those days there wasn't a great deal to do, with only five tables overlooking the vineyards and deck. Now there are more than eighty tables in the lovely new restaurant and coach house, plus a year-round calendar of special events and festivities. A chef who prefers to enhance rather than camouflage his ingredients, Mark has emerged as a champion of Niagara's seasonal produce.

Wine Suggestions
Canadian Sauvignon Blanc
Californian Sauvignon Blanc
The dominant flavour here is asparagus. Sauvignon Blanc will complement its unique taste.

Toasted Sesame Rice Cakes with Asparagus Ice

Serve this subtle dish as an intermezzo between dishes as part of a tasting menu or as an unusual first course. Use Japanese medium-grain rice to achieve the stickiness needed to hold the cakes together.

ASPARAGUS ICE:
4 cups table cream
7 egg yolks
½ cup granulated sugar
½ tsp kosher salt
1½ cups asparagus tips

SESAME RICE CAKES:
1 cup Japanese rice
1½ cups cold water
1 cup mirin (Japanese rice wine)
2 drops orange oil (optional)
2 tbsp toasted sesame seeds

Heat cream in saucepan just until steaming and bubbles form around edge.

Whisk together egg yolks and sugar in bowl. In slow, steady stream, whisk in hot cream. Rinse saucepan and return cream mixture to pan. Cook over medium-low heat, stirring constantly, for 10 to 15 minutes or until thick enough to coat spoon. Cool.

Add salt to saucepan of water and bring to boil. Add asparagus and cook for about 7 minutes or until very tender. Drain, refresh with cold water and puree in food processor until smooth, adding tablespoon of cooking water if needed.

Whisk asparagus puree into custard and refrigerate until chilled and thickened, about 4 hours or overnight.

Freeze asparagus custard in ice-cream maker according to manufacturer's instructions. (To make ice cream without ice-cream maker, freeze in metal bowl, then process in food processor until fairly smooth. Return to freezer and freeze until needed.)

Bring rice and water to boil in saucepan. Reduce heat and simmer, covered, for 25 minutes or until water is absorbed and rice is tender. Transfer rice to large bowl.

Toss warm rice with mirin, orange oil and sesame seeds. Set aside to cool. Shape rice into 12 discs. Serve with asparagus ice on top.

Makes 12 servings.

Main Courses

BANGKOK GARDEN [PAYOONG KLINPROONG]

When Sherry Brydson built Bangkok Garden at the foot of the Elmwood Club in 1982, she helped start a vogue for Thai cuisine that remains with us still. Buddhist monks blessed the premises; incense still curls from the spirit house in the entry. The dining room is an elaborate space, fashioned from a forest of teak. Brydson also brought a chef from Thailand, Payoong Klinproong, who was willing and able to temper the sour heat of some (but not all) of her recipes to Canadian palates. Even now, when so much water has passed under the restaurant's ornamental bridge, dining at Bangkok Garden remains an exotic adventure.

ROASTED RICE POWDER

Heat wok or saucepan over high heat until smoking. Add ¼ cup uncooked rice and cook, stirring, for 2 minutes or until golden. Transfer to bowl and cool. With mortar and pestle or in clean coffee grinder, grind rice to a consistency between coarse and fine ground pepper. Store at room temperature in tightly covered jar.

WINE SUGGESTIONS
Canadian dry Riesling 🍁
Alsace Riesling
The tartness and sweet mix of flavours call for a wine with lively acidity and a touch of residual sugar.

Royal Barge

This salad makes an interesting main course served over leaf lettuce and accompanied by sticky rice or rice noodles. You could also serve a cucumber salad on the side instead of making the "barge."

1 lb beef tenderloin
1 tbsp vegetable oil
6 tbsp lemon juice
2 tbsp Thai fish sauce
1½ tsp granulated sugar
1 tsp Asian chili sauce, or more to taste
¼ cup chopped fresh coriander

¼ cup chopped fresh mint
2 shallots, finely chopped
2 green onions, chopped
1 tbsp ground roasted rice (optional)
2 field cucumbers, halved lengthwise and
   carved into "boats"

Brush beef with oil and place on grill over medium-high heat. Close lid and grill for 20 minutes, turning every 5 minutes, until medium-rare. Cool.

Whisk together lemon juice, fish sauce, sugar and chili sauce in small bowl.

Cut beef crosswise into slices ¼ inch thick. Stack slices and cut into ¼-inch strips.

Place beef in bowl with coriander, mint, shallots, green onions and roasted rice powder if using. Add dressing and toss to coat. Divide among cucumber boats.

Makes 4 servings.

CANOE

[Todd Clarmo and Anthony Walsh]

High above the city on the fifty-fourth floor of the Toronto-Dominion tower, in a room full of light, stands Canoe. Together with Jump and Auberge du Pommier, it forms part of the triple crown worn by restaurateurs Peter Oliver and Michael Bonacini, beloved by downtown suits and by anyone else who enjoys excellent food with a clever Canadian theme. Jeff Dueck was the first chef here, back in 1995. When he left, Oliver and Bonacini promoted from within, giving the kitchen to a team of two young Canadian chefs, Todd Clarmo and Anthony Walsh. They rose brilliantly to the challenge. These days they ride between the three restaurants, going wherever they are needed, doing what must be done to maintain the high standards that Oliver and Bonacini set.

ACHIOTE

Achiote or annatto is a peppery red seed that colours a dish as well as spicing it. It is often used to give Mexican food its characteristic colour and spice. Look for it in Mexican, South American and Caribbean stores.

WINE SUGGESTIONS

BC Ehrenfelser or Ontario Scheurebe 🍁
off-dry Vouvray (Loire) or Rheingau Riesling Spätlese (Germany)
The sweetness of the dish requires a white wine with some residual sugar but good balancing acidity.

BEER SUGGESTION

Bock
A little sweetness, a little spice, a rich aroma and flavour; a good bock will echo and accentuate all the qualities of this dish

Spiced Maple Barbecued Sweetbreads with Charred Green Tomato Pickle

Serve these with soft pitas or other flatbread to complement the pungent tomato pickle and the spicy, crusty sweetbreads. To grill the tomato, cut in half and grill or broil until the skin is charred. If you prefer, substitute chicken for the sweetbreads.

SWEETBREADS:
1 lb veal sweetbreads (page 37), soaked
    overnight and well rinsed
½ cup olive oil
3 tbsp achiote spice (annatto paste)
2 tbsp paprika
2 tbsp chopped fresh rosemary or 2 tsp dried
2 tbsp chopped fresh thyme or 2 tsp dried
2 tbsp maple syrup
1 jalapeño pepper, seeded and finely chopped
Salt to taste
1 tbsp coarsely ground pepper

TOMATO PICKLE:
¼ cup red wine vinegar
¼ cup finely chopped shallots
2 tbsp granulated sugar
Salt to taste
2 tbsp sherry vinegar
1 green tomato, grilled and diced
1 red tomato, diced
¼ cup olive oil
¼ cup chopped fresh parsley

Cover sweetbreads with cold water in saucepan. Bring to boil and simmer for 15 minutes. Drain and place on plate. Cover with second plate weighted with cans for 1 hour. Discard any liquid. Remove any sinew and membrane.

Heat ½ cup olive oil in small saucepan over medium heat. Add achiote and cook, stirring, until aromatic, about 1 minute. Remove from heat and stir in paprika, rosemary, thyme, maple syrup, jalapeño, salt and pepper.

Place sweetbreads in shallow dish. Pour spice mixture over, turning sweetbreads to coat evenly. Cover and refrigerate for 2 to 6 hours.

Whisk together wine vinegar, shallots, sugar, salt and sherry vinegar in bowl. Let stand for 30 minutes. Stir in green and red tomato, ¼ cup oil and parsley.

Grill sweetbreads for 15 minutes, turning once, until blackened and centre is tender and cooked through. Slice sweetbreads and serve with tomato pickle.

Makes 4 servings.

CHIADO [ALBINO SILVA AND MANUEL VILELA]

Albino Silva's story reads a little like a romance. He learned to cook as a child on his family's farm in the Trás-os-Montes region of Portugal, then apprenticed in his father's pastry shop in Lisbon. By the age of fourteen he was a qualified pastry chef—then the family moved to Toronto. At seventeen, still in grade eleven, he was chef of The Cossacks, a dazzlingly up-scale Russian restaurant; ten years later he joined the faculty of the Culinary Institute of America, teaching his own course in restaurant etiquette, protocol and manners. Happily, he decided to return to Toronto and eventually opened Chiado. The food and the wine list have been a revelation—Portuguese haute cuisine of a quality undreamed of in Hogtown, with a menu that sometimes includes the dishes he learned on the family farm. Since then, Silva has opened or helped to create other restaurants—Adega, Boémia, Circo—but Chiado remains his masterpiece, an embassy of Lusitanian culture.

WINE SUGGESTIONS
Canadian off-dry Riesling 🍁
California Chenin Blanc or Alsace Riesling
The hot spicy sausages dominate here, so match with an off-dry white wine with lively acidity.

Clams with Chourico

This classic Portuguese dish should be served with lots of crusty bread to mop up the savoury sauce. Chourico is a spicy smoked pork sausage (known as chorizo in Spanish cooking); it may be salty, so taste before adding any extra salt to this dish.

¼ cup olive oil
3 Spanish onions, thinly sliced
3 large cloves garlic, finely chopped
2 large sweet red peppers, cut in thin strips
1 large bay leaf
1 28-oz/796 mL can tomatoes, pureed with juices

1 chourico sausage, skin removed and diced
Pinch hot red pepper flakes
4 dozen small clams, rinsed
¼ cup dry white wine
¼ cup coarsely chopped fresh parsley

Heat oil in large heavy skillet over medium heat. Cook onions, garlic and peppers, stirring, for about 10 minutes or until limp and tinged with gold.

Add bay leaf and tomatoes and bring to boil. Reduce heat and simmer, covered, for 30 minutes.

Add chourico and hot pepper flakes. Simmer for 30 minutes longer.

Spoon half the tomato mixture into bottom of shallow Dutch oven. Bring to simmer over medium heat. Arrange clams on top (discard any clams that do not close when tapped). Spoon in remaining tomato sauce. Cover and cook for a few minutes or until sauce returns to simmer.

Pour in wine and parsley and toss with clams. Cook, covered, for 10 to 15 minutes longer or until clams open. Discard any clams that do not open. Discard bay leaf before serving.

Makes 6 servings.

XAVIER DESHAYES

Born in the Roussillon region, Xavier Deshayes came to Toronto in 1994 to take on the challenging role of restaurant chef at Truffles, signature dining room of the Four Seasons Hotel. His experience included time at Citron in Los Angeles and at Le Manoir aux Quat' Saisons in England; he was young, energetic and very, very good. Within a month or two, he and executive chef, Denis Jaricot, had embarked on a series of menus to showcase the cuisine of seven French regions, but he was also delighted to emerge from the kitchen and discuss what an individual customer might feel like eating that night. As time passed, he began to expand his repertoire, working brilliantly with North American notions and ingredients. Right now he is chef and partner at Sen5es Restaurant and Bakery in Washington D.C., but he still comes back to Toronto occasionally for guest appearances—evenings his many fans wait for with greedy anticipation.

WINE SUGGESTIONS
Canadian Sauvignon Blanc 🍁
Pouilly-Fumé (Loire) or white Rhône
A plethora of flavours and textures here: you can go either white or red with bold, dry wines.

Provençal Paella of Seafood and Pearl Pasta

provençal paella

This wonderful mixture of pasta and seafood is a colourful and light main course. Vary the vegetables and the seafood according to your own taste.

2 to 3 cups chicken stock
6 cloves garlic, finely chopped
Pinch saffron threads
2 tbsp olive oil
1 onion, diced
1 bulb fennel, diced
1 artichoke heart, diced
1 yellow zucchini, diced
1 green zucchini, diced
½ eggplant, peeled and diced
½ sweet green pepper, diced

½ sweet red pepper, diced
6 plum tomatoes, seeded and diced
1 cup Israeli couscous
8 mussels, rinsed
8 clams, rinsed
8 large shrimp, peeled and deveined
8 scallops, rinsed
8 oz salmon fillet, cubed
8 oz red snapper fillet, cubed
Salt and freshly ground pepper to taste

Combine 2 cups chicken stock, garlic and saffron in large saucepan.

Heat oil in large skillet over medium-high heat. One at a time, lightly brown onion, fennel, artichoke, zucchini and eggplant, about 5 minutes each.

Add all vegetables to stock with peppers, tomatoes, pasta, mussels, clams and shrimp. Bring to boil, reduce heat and simmer for 5 minutes.

Add scallops, salmon and snapper. Add more stock if necessary. Season with salt and pepper. Cook for 5 to 8 minutes or until seafood is just cooked.

Makes 4 servings.

GALLERY GRILL AT HART HOUSE

[SUZANNE BABY]

PEPPERED CHERRIES

Combine ¼ cup dry red wine, 2 tbsp Port, 2 tbsp granulated sugar and 2 tbsp red wine vinegar in small saucepan. Tie 2 tbsp cracked black peppercorns, ¼ cinnamon stick and 1 tbsp anise seeds in cheesecloth and add to saucepan. Bring to boil. Pour mixture over ½ cup pitted cherries in small jar. Cover and refrigerate for 2 to 3 weeks.

Makes about ¾ cup.

The Grill really is a gallery—a handsome, vaulted clerestory above the neo-Gothic Great Hall of Hart House at the University of Toronto. Once it had been a student club, but Peter Turner, warden of Hart House, saw its future in broader terms. He turned to Bob Sniderman of the Senator to help create the Grill, and Sniderman brought in chef Suzanne Baby, formerly of Lakes and Acqua, and sous-chef Caroline Simpson. Open to students and the public alike, it instantly became known as one of the most original and delicious lunch spots in Toronto. Baby weaves all sorts of subtle culinary allusions into her fresh, imaginative dishes; in her hands, even an apparently simple appetizer becomes a little work of art, an educative lesson in pleasure—which couldn't be more appropriate.

WINE SUGGESTIONS
Canadian Pinot Noir 🍁
Oregon or California Pinot Noir
If ever there was a marriage made in heaven, it's duck with Pinot Noir—in this case a New World style Pinot Noir.

Duck Confit Cakes with Peppered Cherries

It is possible to buy prepared duck confit at better butchers and some supermarkets, but true duck lovers will really appreciate this dish. If you do not have enough duck fat (it can also be purchased) add lard or shortening. The duck meat doesn't have to be formed into cakes—you can simply broil the duck legs. Lay on a baking sheet and broil until the skin crisps and legs are warm.

Use dried cherries if fresh are unavailable. Classic accompaniments for this dish include red cabbage or a salad of frisee lettuce.

---

2 lb duck legs
1 onion, coarsely chopped
8 cloves garlic, chopped
2 sprigs fresh rosemary, coarsely chopped
6 sprigs thyme, coarsely chopped
4 bay leaves
½ cup coarse salt

1 tbsp whole peppercorns
1 cinnamon stick, broken in pieces
5 star anise
1 tsp fennel seeds
4 cups rendered duck fat
2 tbsp roasted garlic puree (page 94)
½ tsp chopped fresh thyme or pinch dried

Place duck legs in shallow baking dish.

Combine onion, chopped garlic, rosemary, thyme sprigs, bay leaves, salt, peppercorns, cinnamon stick, star anise and fennel seeds in bowl.

Coat duck with herb mixture and cover with plastic wrap. Weight down duck legs using heavy cans or plates and refrigerate overnight. Brush off excess herb mixture.

Melt duck fat over low heat in wok or saucepan large enough to hold duck legs. Add duck and cook, uncovered, for about 3 hours or until very tender. The fat should barely bubble. Refrigerate legs in fat for 2 to 3 weeks to allow flavour to mature.

Remove skin and bones from duck, shred meat and place in bowl. Add roasted garlic and thyme.

Form meat mixture into 4 cakes, pressing together. Heat 1 tbsp duck fat in non-stick skillet on medium-high heat and cook duck cakes for 4 minutes, turning once, until golden brown on each side. Serve duck cakes with peppered cherries (page 92).

Makes 4 servings.

HEMISPHERES

[NEAL NOBLE]

Neal Noble can't help but chuckle as he looks back on his past career moves. "I was born and raised in Fort Frances, Ontario, but I did my training in Vancouver and I've been working my way back east ever since." That work includes eight years at the Sutton Place Hotel in Toronto, "in the wild and crazy days of Sanssouci restaurant," before he joined the Metropolitan Hotel in 1996. Today, as corporate executive chef, his responsibilities are awe-inspiring, covering not only the hotel's restaurants but also the Sen5es restaurants in Toronto and Washington D.C. and Sen5es fine food store on Bloor Street. There, amidst all the exquisitely packaged gourmet delights, one might be lucky enough to find his prepared foie gras, a crucial ingredient of Tournedos Rossini.

ROASTED GARLIC PUREE

To roast garlic, cut ½ inch from top of garlic head to expose cloves. Remove any excess papery skin from head, but do not peel. Sprinkle garlic with 1 tsp olive oil and wrap in foil. Bake in a preheated 400°F oven for 40 to 45 minutes or until very soft. Cool. Squeeze garlic out of cloves from base and discard skins.

Makes about 2 tbsp puree.

WINE SUGGESTIONS
Canadian Syrah 🍁
California Zinfandel or Australian Shiraz
The foie gras adds richness to the beef so look for a hefty red wine with forward fruit.

Tournedos Rossini with Welsh Griddle Cakes

The texture and taste combinations in this dish are unusual and superb—the meat is slightly salty, the foie gras meltingly soft. Serve it as a first course with the griddle cakes, or as a main course with rosti potatoes and braised endive. If you can't find lavender jelly, use another herb-flavoured jelly.

WELSH GRIDDLE CAKES:
2 cups all-purpose flour
1 tbsp baking powder
½ tsp granulated sugar
½ tsp salt
1 cup plus 2 tbsp milk
⅓ cup currants
2 tsp chopped fresh thyme
    (preferably lemon thyme)
1 tbsp vegetable oil
¼ cup lavender jelly

TOURNEDOS:
1 lb centre-cut beef tenderloin,
    cut lengthwise in quarters
2 tbsp roasted garlic puree (page 94)
4 oz foie gras
Salt and freshly ground pepper to taste
1 tbsp vegetable oil

Sift together flour, baking powder, sugar and salt in bowl. Stir in milk to make soft batter. Fold in currants and thyme.

Heat 1 tbsp oil in large skillet over medium-high heat. Spoon batter into skillet in 2-inch rounds and cook until edges start to dry out. Turn and cook for 1 minute longer. Repeat with remaining batter and oil.

Remove hot griddle cakes to baking sheet and brush immediately with lavender jelly.

Preheat oven to 350°F. Cover beef with parchment paper and pound to ¼-inch thickness. Spread each piece with roasted garlic and foie gras and season lightly with salt and pepper. Roll each piece of beef into tight cylinder and tie every inch with butcher's twine.

Heat 1 tbsp oil in ovenproof skillet over high heat. Sear beef until well browned, about 1 minute per side. Transfer skillet to oven and roast for 10 minutes. Remove strings and slice each cylinder into 4 rounds.

Reheat griddle cakes in oven and serve topped with slices of beef.

Makes 4 servings.

HERBS

[ANTHONY NUTH]

If you ever come across a copy of an English recipe book called *My Gastronomy*, written by London superchef Nico Ladenis, look closely at the photographs. They show a young Tony Nuth, deep in concentration, preparing some of the dishes in Ladenis's restaurant kitchen. Nuth had left Canada to finish his gastronomic education, the seeds of which bore delicious fruit when he came back and opened Herbs, on Yonge Street, in 1993. It was the precision of his technique and the clarity of his flavours that raised the cooking high above the bistro norm. Then there were the sophisticated classics that graced the menu—succulent pheasant confit, a ballotine of chicken in a sauce of morels and cream, followed by a spectacularly good lemon tart. Herbs has prospered and, a couple of years ago, Nuth and his team opened a café and fine food store across the street. Now Lawrence Park gourmets have somewhere to shop as well as somewhere to dine.

WINE SUGGESTIONS
Canadian off-dry Riesling
German Riesling Spätlese
The Thai spicing calls for a white wine with some residual sweetness and good balancing acidity.

Grilled Ontario Pork Tenderloin with Japanese Eggplant Caviar

Serve the pork with stir-fried mixed vegetables and steamed rice flavoured with ginger and coriander.

- -

FRIED WONTONS:
Vegetable oil for deep-frying
18 3-inch wonton wrappers

PORK:
¼ cup soy sauce
¼ cup sesame oil
2 tbsp honey
1½ tbsp grated ginger

1 shallot, finely chopped
1 tsp chopped and seeded jalapeño pepper
1 tbsp chopped fresh coriander
2 10-oz pork tenderloins

JAPANESE EGGPLANT CAVIAR:
6 Japanese eggplants
4 tbsp light miso paste
½ cup chicken stock

- -

Heat vegetable oil in wok or deep skillet to 360°F (or until a cube of bread turns brown in 30 seconds). Add wonton wrappers to oil in batches and fry until golden, about 1 minute. Drain on paper towels.

Whisk soy sauce, sesame oil, honey, ginger, shallot, jalapeño and coriander in small bowl. Pour over pork in shallow dish, turning to coat well. Cover and refrigerate for 12 hours.

Preheat oven to 400°F.

Cut each eggplant in half lengthwise. Place skin side down on baking sheet and roast for 25 minutes or until soft. Let cool slightly. Scoop out flesh and transfer to food processor.

Add miso and puree until smooth and well blended, adding up to ½ cup stock to make mixture as smooth as possible. Cool.

Bring pork to room temperature for 30 minutes. Grill or barbecue pork, turning frequently until just a hint of pink remains, about 15 to 20 minutes. Baste with marinade every 5 minutes during cooking.

Place wonton wrappers in oven for 2 minutes to reheat.

Cut tenderloins into thin rounds. Place 3 wontons on each plate and top with overlapping slices of pork. Top with eggplant.

Makes 6 servings.

INDIAN RICE FACTORY [MRS. AMAR PATEL]

In 1967, Mrs. Amar Patel, a young registered nurse from Bombay, accepted an invitation from the French kitchen team at the Inn on the Park who wanted her to teach them how to prepare real Indian food. Three years later she opened a restaurant of her own, Indian Rice Factory, on Dupont. Cooked à la minute, in full view of her customers, Mrs. Patel's dishes broke the mould of the generic Indian restaurant menu. They still do so today. Now her son, Aman, manages the room, finding fine wines that work wonderfully well with his mother's cooking. The job she began thirty-three years ago is not yet over. She is still educating our palates, teaching us, dish by dish, about the endless culinary subtleties of the subcontinent.

WINE SUGGESTIONS
A dry Canadian Gewürztraminer ❦
Alsace Gewürztraminer or dry Muscat
A highly spiced dish so mellow it with a voluptuous Gewürztraminer.

BEER SUGGESTION
Märzen
The crisp character and light spiciness of this German-style lager make it a natural for chicken and a refreshing complement to this dish.

Chicken Tikka

There is increased interest today in spicy foods and fragrant flavours. Indian food is both these things and more. Serve this dish with basmati rice flavoured with saffron, naan bread and thinly sliced onions tossed with lemon juice and black pepper.

1 lb boneless skinless chicken breasts
¼ cup yogurt
1 tbsp finely chopped garlic
1 tbsp grated ginger
1 tbsp lemon juice

1 tsp garam masala
1 tsp ground cumin
Pinch cayenne
Pinch ground fenugreek (optional)
Salt to taste

Place chicken breasts between two sheets of plastic wrap and pound until ½ inch thick.

Combine yogurt, garlic, ginger, lemon juice, garam masala, cumin, cayenne, fenugreek and salt in large bowl. Add chicken pieces and toss to coat. Cover with plastic wrap and refrigerate overnight.

Remove chicken from marinade. Grill on lightly oiled grill pan over medium-high heat or broil for about 3 to 4 minutes per side or until no longer pink inside.

Makes 4 servings.

MASTRO'S

[RINA CAMARRA]

PECORINO

Pecorino cheese is a hard, sharp-flavoured, salty sheep's milk cheese. It is usually used grated and is an essential ingredient in southern Italian cooking. If you can't find it, substitute another hard cheese such as Parmesan.

What is it about Mastro's that has kept generations of restaurant-goers coming back time and again for more than thirty years? The comfortable calm of those panelled rooms? A wine list laden with noble Italian producers and famous vintages? Or is it the sophisticated little touches that bring the traditional Italian menu to life — the quality and freshness of the golden chicken stock in a simple soup; the rich, well-balanced sauces; the ungussied perfection of a dish of grilled seafood; the delicious variety of the antipasto. Order the cheese plate and great chunks of prime Parmigiano Reggiano, Asiago and pecorino appear, from which customers can carve as much or as little as they please. These are the secrets of longevity.

WINE SUGGESTIONS
Ontario Gamay Noir or BC Pinot Gris 🍁
Beaujolais, Chianti Classico or Pouilly-Fumé (Loire)
Pork has intrinsic sweetness but the spinach and cheese add flavours that make this dish better suited to a wine with good acidity.

Stuffed Pork Tenderloins

An interesting and different Italian-flavoured pork dish. Serve with roasted red potatoes.

---

10 oz fresh spinach	2 1-lb pork tenderloins
1 cup ricotta cheese	⅓ cup all-purpose flour
¼ cup grated pecorino cheese	¼ cup olive oil
1 egg, lightly beaten	1 small onion, chopped
Salt, freshly ground pepper and	1 cup dry red wine
grated nutmeg to taste	1 cup chicken stock

Preheat oven to 400°F.

Rinse spinach and remove stems. Place in saucepan on medium heat with water clinging to spinach leaves. Cover and cook for 1 to 2 minutes until wilted. Drain, rinse with cold water and squeeze out excess moisture. Chop finely.

Combine spinach with ricotta, pecorino and egg in bowl. Add salt, pepper and nutmeg.

Butterfly each tenderloin, leaving one long side attached.

Spread spinach mixture down centre of each tenderloin. Fold tenderloins and tie or skewer to close. Roll tenderloins in flour.

Heat oil in large ovenproof skillet on medium-high heat. Add onion and season with salt and pepper. Add tenderloins and season with salt and pepper. Cook until golden brown all over, about 5 to 7 minutes. Pour off excess oil and add red wine. Cover and place in oven for 20 minutes or until juices are clear.

Remove tenderloins from pan and keep warm. Place pan on medium-high heat. Add stock and cook until pan juices are reduced and thickened, about 8 to 10 minutes.

Slice tenderloins on the diagonal. Arrange slices on serving platter. Strain reduced pan juices and drizzle over meat.

Makes 4 to 6 servings.

MILLIE'S BISTRO

[GARY HOYER]

PRESERVED LEMONS

Lemons pickled in salt and lemon juice are used as an ingredient and garnish in many Moroccan recipes. They have an amazing flavour that cannot be duplicated by fresh lemons. To prepare them, scrub 3 lemons and dry well. Cut each into 8 wedges but leave attached at one end. Place in glass jar with glass or plastic lid. Mix about 1/3 cup coarse sea salt and 1/2 cup lemon juice and pour over lemons. Cover and let sit at room temperature for one week, shaking jar each day to distribute salt and juice. Cover with olive oil and refrigerate for up to 6 months.

To use, cut off pulp and discard, then slice rind thinly.

Few if any chefs in Toronto take such pains to source and use prime local organic produce as Gary Hoyer. Baskets and bushels of ripe fruit and vegetables stand in front of the open kitchen at his restaurant, Millie's Bistro, up on Avenue Road—for sale, if you wish, or better yet for use in the dishes he puts on the menu. The entire Mediterranean rim is his oyster, with forays inland into Morocco or up around the Black Sea, while his style is always admirably clear and fresh flavoured. But that's what Toronto has come to expect from Gary Hoyer. From his early days at the Windsor Arms, Biffi Bistro and Le Gourmet, through Amsterdam, Tutto Bene, Mezzo and now at Millie's, his originality has shone forth on the plate. Vegetarians, in particular, have delighted in the loving care he lavishes on the humblest cabbage, the smallest chickpea. Who is Millie? Take a look at a bag of Millie's Cosmic Chips, the yummy organic root vegetable crisps Gary makes and sells. That cheerful little dog on the packet is Millie herself.

WINE SUGGESTIONS

Ontario Sauvignon Blanc or BC Pinot Gris ❧
California Sauvignon Blanc
Exotic spicing for a vegetable dish—the best bet is Sauvignon Blanc with its green veggie flavours, but choose one with ripe fruit flavours to balance the spices.

B'stilla with Wild Leeks and Ricotta

In Morocco, b'stilla is a special-occasion dish. It is traditionally made with pigeons, but this is a vegetarian version.

¾ cup butter
2 lb wild leeks (page 110) or 5 regular leeks (white part only), thinly sliced
½ tsp saffron threads
½ tsp turmeric
1 cinnamon stick
Salt and freshly ground pepper to taste
1¼ cups vegetable stock
1 cup ricotta cheese

1 large Spanish onion, thickly sliced
3 cloves garlic, chopped
1 cup chopped fresh parsley
½ cup lemon juice
8 eggs, beaten
12 oz phyllo pastry
¼ tsp cinnamon
½ preserved lemon, finely chopped

Melt ¼ cup butter in large skillet over medium heat. Add leeks, half the saffron, half the turmeric, cinnamon stick, salt and pepper. Cook, stirring occasionally, for 15 minutes or until soft.

Add stock and simmer for 10 minutes. Remove leeks with slotted spoon. Reserve stock in skillet and discard cinnamon stick. Cool leeks slightly and mix with ricotta in large bowl until well combined. Season to taste with salt and pepper.

Reduce reserved stock to ½ cup on high heat. Add onion, garlic, parsley and remaining saffron and turmeric.

Reduce heat to medium-low and cook for about 30 minutes or until onions are consistency of marmalade. Stir in lemon juice and eggs. Cook, stirring, until eggs are cooked, about 3 minutes. Place in sieve to drain and discard liquid.

Preheat oven to 425°F. Melt remaining ½ cup butter.

Layer 6 phyllo sheets on baking sheet, spreading each layer with butter. Spread leek mixture over centre of pastry, leaving 1-inch border on all sides. Sprinkle with cinnamon. Spoon egg mixture over top and sprinkle with preserved lemon.

Brush remaining 6 phyllo sheets with butter and lay on top of filling. Fold edges of phyllo under to make tightly closed packet. Drizzle with remaining butter and bake for about 25 minutes or until golden brown. Cut into slices to serve.

Makes 6 servings.

MISTURA

"Oh, this sea bass, this sea bass," says Massimo Capra in a voice half laughter and half rueful sigh. "It's so popular. There'd be a riot if I ever tried to take it off the menu." The menu in question is that of Mistura, the hugely popular restaurant that chef Massimo created with his partner, front-of-house maestro Paolo Paolini. Sea bass aside, Mistura's card is full of the robust flavours and hearty northern Italian cooking that Capra grew up with in his native Cremona. He might have stayed there if a cousin hadn't opened Archer's in Toronto and asked him to be chef. He came over in 1982 and has been here ever since, working for many years with Michael Carlevale at Prego della Piazza until he left for Mistura two years ago.

WINE SUGGESTIONS
Canadian off-dry Riesling 🍁
German Riesling Kabinett or Alsace Tokay-Pinot Gris
The ginger soy sauce adds a piquant note that suggests a fruity white wine
with a little residual sweetness and good acidity.

Chilean Black Sea Bass with Mustard Crust and Ginger Soy Mirin Sauce

The sweet and hot crust goes beautifully with the rich, deep sauce.

---

4 Chilean black sea bass fillets (6 oz each)
Salt and freshly ground pepper to taste
1 tbsp vegetable oil
¼ cup grainy Dijon mustard
2 tbsp chopped pickled ginger
1 tbsp roasted garlic puree (page 94)

GINGER SOY MIRIN SAUCE:
1 tbsp vegetable oil
1 onion, thinly sliced
¼ cup grated ginger

10 dried shiitake mushrooms, soaked in hot water
    for 20 minutes, stemmed and thinly sliced
3 sweet apples (e.g., McIntosh or Royal Gala),
    peeled and chopped
3 cloves garlic, sliced
3 stalks lemongrass, finely chopped
1 carrot, chopped
¼ cup mirin (Japanese rice wine)
¼ cup light soy sauce
1 cup vegetable or chicken stock
Black and white toasted sesame seeds

Preheat oven to 450°F. Rinse fish and pat dry. Sprinkle with salt and pepper.

Heat 1 tbsp oil in large skillet on high heat. Cook fish for 2 minutes per side.

Puree mustard, pickled ginger and roasted garlic in food processor or blender. Spread over top of fish and place fish on baking sheet.

Heat 1 tbsp oil in saucepan on medium heat. Add onion and cook until soft, about 5 minutes. Add grated ginger, mushrooms, apples, sliced garlic, lemongrass and carrot and cook for 5 to 7 minutes, stirring, until soft.

Add mirin and reduce by half, about 1 minute. Stir in soy sauce and stock. Bring to boil and reduce by half, about 5 minutes.

Drain apple mixture in strainer, pressing down with spoon to press out all liquid. Return liquid to saucepan and reheat when needed.

Bake fish for 10 to 12 minutes or until just cooked. Sprinkle with sesame seeds and serve with sauce.

Makes 4 servings.

NORTH 44°

[MARK McEWAN]

Overnight sensation. That was the word on Mark McEwan when he suddenly became executive chef of the Sutton Place Hotel at the tender age of twenty-five. Never mind that he had spent seven years at the Constellation Hotel, working his way from apprentice to sous-chef under the tutelage of the legendary Joseph Vonlanthen. McEwan was a golden boy—more so when he and his partners took over Pronto in 1985, and even more so when he created North 44°. Ten years on, the restaurant has never looked better or run so smoothly, with every minuscule nuance of food and service reflecting McEwan's high-resolution focus. Young cooks who fail to last the course in his kitchen moan about demands to excel; those who make the grade emerge with a rare grounding in every aspect of restaurant cooking. Relentless energy, ceaseless movement: these are the dynamics that produce the sense of calm stability his customers have come to expect. And dishes that show off the quality of his ingredients, with nods to Asia and the Mediterranean, but never with gimmicks or games of hide and seek. "I don't like food that is overspun," says McEwan. "If I serve lamb, I want it to taste of lamb." And it does. Gloriously.

WINE SUGGESTIONS
BC Merlot or Ontario Cabernet Franc 🍁
California Cabernet Sauvignon or Merlot
The classic match for lamb is red Bordeaux but the crusting suggests a
New World Merlot or Cab with a touch of sweetness in the fruit.

Rack of Lamb with Pecan Honey Mustard Crust and Green Onion Mint Pesto

Use fresh Australian or local lamb in this recipe if you can, and ask your butcher to french the rack by removing the chine bone and cleaning the bones up to the eye of the meat. This makes an elegant presentation and allows diners to pick up the bones cleanly.

2 racks of lamb (about 1¼ lb each)
2 tbsp olive oil
2 tsp chopped fresh thyme or ½ tsp dried
1 tbsp honey
1 tbsp Dijon mustard
Salt and freshly ground pepper to taste
3 tbsp chopped toasted pecans
1 cup fresh sourdough breadcrumbs, toasted
1 tbsp melted butter

GREEN ONION MINT PESTO:
6 green onions, trimmed
½ cup fresh mint leaves
½ cup rice vinegar
1 tbsp toasted pine nuts
1 tsp granulated sugar
1 tsp grated lemon rind
1 tsp finely chopped jalapeño pepper
Salt to taste

Preheat oven to 400°F. Drizzle lamb with 1 tbsp oil and rub with thyme.

Heat remaining 1 tbsp oil in large ovenproof skillet over high heat. Brown lamb on all sides, about 4 minutes. Place skillet in oven and roast lamb for 10 minutes.

Stir together honey, mustard, salt and pepper in small bowl.

Combine pecans and breadcrumbs in separate bowl.

Spread lamb with honey mixture, then coat with breadcrumb mixture, letting excess fall into skillet. Drizzle with melted but-

ter. Return to oven and roast for another 15 to 20 minutes, or until desired doneness. Let rest, covered, for about 5 minutes.

Puree green onions, mint, vinegar, pine nuts, sugar, lemon rind, jalapeño and salt in food processor. Adjust seasoning to taste.

Slice lamb between bones. Serve with pesto.

Makes 4 servings.

ON THE TWENTY [MICHAEL OLSON]

Len Pennachetti acquires a century-old building in the sleepy village of Jordan on the Niagara peninsula, a building the size of a city block, big enough to house his newly formed Cave Spring Cellars winery and then some. With his wife, Helen Young, he decides to invent a restaurant, a place that will showcase the fabulous produce of Niagara, that will pioneer a wine country cuisine, that will give wine pilgrims a reason to linger in Jordan. Chef Michael Olson, formerly of Liberty, now working in Ottawa, is soon brought on board and enters into the plan with alacrity. He gets on his bike and visits the local farmers, winning them over, placing orders for pears or peaches or peppers or quail and using these prime ingredients as nature, and Len and Helen, intended. The restaurant, called On the Twenty, quickly acquires a golden reputation and soon other wineries embrace the vision, bringing in talented chefs and building beautiful dining rooms. While Olson generously shares his contacts and advice, On The Twenty remains the place where our wine country cooking began, the flagship of Niagara's burgeoning culinary identity.

WINE SUGGESTIONS
Ontario Chardonnay 🍁
California or Australian Chardonnay
Sweet and spicy sauce and hot relish point to a barrel-fermented Chardonnay with lots of fruit extract (for lovers of red, go Amarone or full-blooded Zinfandel).

Ontario Pork Loin in Maple Beer Sauce with Sweet Pepper Relish

If peaches are out of season, make the relish with mangoes. The fruity, fresh relish can also be served with chicken, ham and other cold meats. Make it a day or two ahead.

SWEET PEPPER RELISH:
1 habañero or Scotch bonnet pepper (page 114), seeded and chopped
6 sweet red peppers, seeded and chopped
6 peaches, peeled and chopped
½ cup white wine vinegar
½ tsp salt
1 lemon, cut in half
½ cup granulated sugar

MAPLE BEER SAUCE:
1 341 mL bottle maple beer
½ onion, diced
3 tart apples (e.g., Mutsu), peeled and sliced
½ cup maple syrup

PORK:
4 lb boneless pork loin, centre cut
2 tbsp chopped fresh thyme or 1 tsp dried
Salt and freshly ground pepper to taste

Combine hot and sweet peppers, peaches, vinegar, salt and lemon in large saucepan. Bring to boil, reduce heat, cover and simmer for 15 minutes. Remove lemon. Stir in sugar and simmer for 30 minutes or until thickened.

Combine beer, onion, apples and maple syrup in separate saucepan. Bring to boil. Reduce heat and cook on medium-low for 30 minutes.

Puree maple-beer mixture in blender and return to saucepan. Cook on medium-low for 10 to 15 minutes or until slightly thickened.

Preheat oven to 450°F. Season pork with thyme, salt and pepper and set in a shallow roasting pan. Pour on sauce and roast for 20 minutes.

Reduce heat to 325°F and roast for 1½ hours until juices run clear or meat thermometer registers 160°F. Let roast rest for 10 minutes before carving. Slice pork and serve with sauce spooned on top. Serve relish on the side.

Makes 12 servings.

OPUS

One of the reasons Michael Stadtländer has exerted such an influence on Canadian cooking is his eye for talent. In the days when he owned Stadtländer's, a young man came looking for work — a giant of a guy with no restaurant experience except a stint as a nightclub bouncer. Michael took him on as an apprentice and Paul Boehmer began to learn. Later he worked at Scaramouche and Bistro 990 before joining forces with his old master once again at Nekah, this time as sous-chef. He came into his own as chef of Opus, the haute location on Prince Arthur Avenue owned by Tony and Mario Amaro. At Taste '99 he chose to prepare a whole roast suckling pig. Even serious foodies blanched to see him twist off its head, but squeams turned to moans of delight when they tasted the incredibly tender meat.

PEELING TOMATOES

To peel tomatoes, score skin and plunge tomatoes in boiling water for 20 seconds. Immerse in cold water. Skins should slip off.

WILD LEEKS

Wild leeks are a delicacy during the spring. Their stalks are streaked with violet and they have broad willowy leaves. They taste of garlic and onion and are quite strong in flavour for such delicate-looking greens.

WINE SUGGESTIONS

Ontario Pinot Noir ❧
Barbaresco (Piedmont) or Chianti Classico Riserva
Tomatoes add acidity to a dish, so look for a red with good acidity as well as fruit.

Grilled Steak with Tomato and Wild Leek Concasse

wild leek concasse

The exotic wild leek concasse is the perfect foil for the earthy flank steak. Serve with a creamy potato gratin.

---

2 tbsp olive oil
1 tbsp cracked black peppercorns
1½ lb flank steak, scored

TOMATO WILD LEEK CONCASSE:
4 ripe tomatoes, peeled, seeded and diced
3 shallots, chopped

⅓ cup chopped wild leeks
   or ½ cup chopped fresh chives
2 tbsp chopped garlic
½ cup olive oil
3 tbsp sherry vinegar
Salt and freshly ground pepper to taste

Combine 2 tbsp oil and cracked pepper in shallow baking dish. Add beef and turn to coat. Cover and refrigerate for 24 hours.

Combine tomatoes, shallots, leeks, garlic, ½ cup oil, vinegar, salt and pepper in bowl. Let stand for 1 hour.

Grill steak on high heat for 5 to 7 minutes per side for rare to medium-rare. Let stand for 10 minutes. Carve steak against grain and serve with spoonful of concasse.

Makes 4 to 6 servings.

IL POSTO NUOVO

[FRANCO AGOSTINO]

Il Posto (Vecchio) had had its day when affable Franco Agostino, consummate host of Forest Hill's local bistro, Banfi, bought the business and added the Nuovo. Redecoration in the dining room and scarily heavy investment in the kitchen further justified the adjective. Suddenly the intimate Italian restaurant on that secluded piazzetta in Hazelton Lanes became one of the most charming places in the city in which to spend an evening. Another reason was the talent of the improbably youthful chef, Bruce Woods. Beaverton born and raised, he trained at Centro with Marc Thuet and then spent a deliciously formative year at Michelin-starred Knockinaam Lodge in remotest Scotland. Equally comfortable with wholesome classics and nifty innovations, Woods gave Il Posto Nuovo a delicious new identity before heading west to Il Giardino in Vancouver.

WINE SUGGESTIONS
Canadian barrel-fermented Chardonnay 🍁
California Chardonnay
A rich dish deserves a buttery Chardonnay.

TRUFFLE OIL

Truffle oil is a big favourite among chefs today. Essentially it is made by infusing olive oil with white truffles. It can be added to a salad dressing for extra richness or drizzled over pasta, soups, vegetables and meats to add a vibrant, elegant flavour. The oil loses its potency after a year, so buy it in small quantities.

Lobster-filled Ravioli with Shrimp and Truffles

If lobster ravioli are unavailable for this sophisticated dish, use mushroom or cheese. Serve as a first course or as a main course with a salad.

---

24 large lobster ravioli
3 tbsp butter
2 tbsp finely chopped shallots
8 shrimp, shelled and chopped

2 tsp chopped black truffles
¼ cup white truffle oil
¼ cup chopped fresh parsley
Salt and freshly ground pepper to taste

Bring salted water to boil in large saucepan. Add ravioli and boil for 4 to 5 minutes or until tender. Drain.

Heat butter in large skillet on medium heat. Add shallots and cook until soft and translucent, about 2 minutes.

Add shrimp and truffles to skillet. Cook for 1 minute until shrimp is bright pink.

Add drained ravioli to skillet and toss, adding up to 2 tbsp pasta water if necessary to create sauce. Add truffle oil and toss to coat ravioli. Stir in parsley, salt and pepper.

Makes 4 servings.

PRONTO RISTORANTE [Annief Coote]

No list of Toronto's most significant restaurants would be complete without Pronto. When Franco Prevedello created it in 1980, he gave the city a new way to dine out, a new style that was glamorous and yet informal, energized instead of sedate. If anything, the energy intensified when he sold the place five years later to Peter Costa, Leslie Kubicek and chef Mark McEwan. The triumvirate had a tough act to follow and plenty to prove. Pronto has been proving it triumphantly ever since, surviving the exit of McEwan, thriving under chefs Dale Nichols, Martin Kouprie, Brad Long and subsequently Annief Coote, who had been there all along, working his way up through the kitchen hierarchy to emerge as a maestro in his own right. Annief is taking a break from cooking these days, but this recipe is typical of the joyously flavourful treats he regularly served at Taste.

SCOTCH BONNET PEPPERS

Scotch bonnets have one of the highest heats on the chili scale. Use rubber gloves to work with the peppers and seed before adding to a recipe. If you want less heat, substitute jalapeños.

WINE SUGGESTIONS
Canadian late harvest Riesling 🍁
California white Zinfandel or late harvest Riesling
A hot and spicy dish so cool your palate with a chilled wine that has some residual sugar.

SCALLOP BOUDIN (PAGE 57)

WHITE CHOCOLATE AND RASPBERRY TART (PAGE 159)

Jerk Chicken Skewers on Grilled Cornbread

grilled cornbread

A savoury mixture of spices gives this chicken major flavour. Buy cornbread, brush with garlic-flavoured oil, grill lightly and serve under chicken with grilled plantain or a green salad alongside.

1½ lb boneless skinless chicken breasts
1 tsp finely chopped Scotch bonnet peppers,
    or to taste
4 cloves garlic, finely chopped
1 tbsp finely chopped fresh thyme or 1 tsp dried

1 tsp freshly ground pepper
½ cup olive oil
Salt to taste
8 slices grilled cornbread

Cut chicken breasts into cubes and place in bowl.

Combine Scotch bonnets, garlic, thyme, pepper, oil and salt in small bowl. Pour over chicken and mix well. Cover and refrigerate overnight.

Soak 4 wooden skewers in water for 30 minutes.

Remove chicken from marinade and skewer.

Grill chicken on medium heat for about 3 minutes per side, basting with marinade during cooking. Serve on grilled cornbread.

Makes 4 servings.

PUSATERI'S

[RICHARD DAUGINIS]

SLOW-ROASTED TOMATOES

Seed and core plum tomatoes. Place tomatoes on an oiled baking sheet and sprinkle with basil, kosher salt and pepper. Sprinkle with a few drops of olive oil and bake in a preheated 275°F oven for about 2 hours or until tomatoes are semi dry. To serve, sauté in more olive oil and drizzle with white wine and balsamic vinegar.

They say a guy once tried to sell Cosmo Pusateri second-rate black truffles. Cosmo picked him up by the scruff of the neck and threw him bodily out of his office. Second-rate anything was not part of the vision Cosmo had nurtured for his beloved store up on Avenue Road, north of Lawrence—a store that he hoped would one day rival Dean & Deluca's in New York and Harrods Food Hall in London. Sensing the coming trend for prepared foods, the store had always made a point of offering a huge range of salads, appetizers and entrees cooked in the busy kitchen behind the meat counter. Well before his untimely death, the shop had entered Toronto's vocabulary as a symbol of high-end food retail, earning special kudos as a generous sponsor of Second Harvest. Last year Pusateri's grew bigger and even more beautiful. Cosmo's dream has come true.

WINE SUGGESTIONS
Canadian Meritage (red Bordeaux blend) or Merlot 🍁
Italian Cabernet Sauvignon or red Bordeaux
A Cabernet Sauvignon-based wine is the perfect match for lamb.

Rack of Lamb Provençal

Serve with slow-roasted plum tomatoes (page 116), Swiss chard and mashed potatoes.

1½ cups fresh breadcrumbs
1 tsp finely chopped garlic
¼ cup chopped tomato
¼ cup chopped fresh parsley
¼ cup chopped fresh thyme
2 tbsp chopped fresh rosemary

Salt and freshly ground pepper to taste
¼ cup clarified butter (page 120)
2 lamb racks, 8 chops each, frenched (page 107)
1 tbsp vegetable oil
2 tbsp Dijon mustard

Combine breadcrumbs, garlic, tomato, parsley, thyme, rosemary, salt, pepper and clarified butter in small bowl.

Preheat oven to 400°F. Season lamb with salt and pepper.

Heat large ovenproof skillet on high heat and add oil. Sear lamb racks, fat side down, for 2 minutes. Turn and sear for 2 more minutes. Upend racks and sear meat ends. Place racks in roasting pan bone side down.

Roast racks for 10 minutes. Remove from oven and brush with mustard. Roll racks in breadcrumb mixture and roast for 10 to 15 minutes or until just pink. Let rest for 5 minutes before carving into chops.

Makes 4 servings.

THE RIVOLI

[WILL LEE, BRENT USPRECH AND PAUL RICKARDS]

Ask four people to describe The Rivoli and you'll probably get four different answers. To some it's a hip club where acts as distinctive as the Cowboy Junkies and Kids in the Hall cut their teeth; to others it's a warm bar and cool pool hall or a favourite patio. Since 1982 it has also been a unique restaurant, famous on Queen Street West for its inventive menus full of exotic Asian references. "The Asian flavours started with our first chef, Vanipha Lana, who had just arrived from Laos," explains co-owner Andre Rosenbaum, "and successive chefs Karen Barnaby, Steve Potovsky and Brad Moore sustained the tradition. The club is a great place for young bands to show off, and the same thing applies to young chefs in our kitchen." Brad Moore had just left for Monsoon when The Rivoli set about creating a dish for Taste '98. Sous-chefs Will Lee, Brent Usprech and Paul Rickards combined their talents to come up with this winning recipe.

WINE SUGGESTIONS
Canadian Syrah 🍁
Australian Shiraz or California Zinfandel
Green chili mint sauce adds a spiciness to the lamb that screams out for
a heavy-duty red.

Pesto-stuffed Lamb Tenderloin with Green Chili Mint Sauce

To butterfly the lamb, cut each loin horizontally through the middle, leaving about ½-inch attached, and open up like a book. Serve with jasmine rice.

4 lamb loins, about 4 oz each, butterflied
2 bunches arugula, roughly chopped
1½ tbsp chopped toasted walnuts
1 tbsp chopped garlic
Salt and freshly ground pepper to taste
3 tbsp olive oil

GREEN CHILI MINT SAUCE:
1 tbsp vegetable oil
2 tsp Asian chili sauce
2 fresh Kaffir lime leaves, chopped,
    or 1 tsp grated lime rind
2 finely chopped cloves garlic

1 shallot, finely chopped
1 tbsp grated ginger
2 tbsp fennel seeds
1 tsp finely chopped lemongrass
2 tbsp dry white wine
¼ cup mirin (Japanese rice wine)
2 tbsp rice vinegar
1 tsp granulated sugar
1 cup water
1 bunch green onions
⅓ cup chopped fresh mint
Salt to taste

Place lamb between 2 sheets of plastic wrap and pound until ¼ inch thick.

Puree arugula, walnuts, chopped garlic, salt, pepper and 2 tbsp olive oil in food processor until smooth. Spread ¼ cup on each lamb loin and roll lengthwise across grain. Cover and refrigerate for 1 hour or overnight.

Heat 1 tbsp vegetable oil on medium heat in saucepan. Add chili sauce, Kaffir leaves, finely chopped garlic, shallot, ginger, fennel seeds and lemongrass and cook for 2 to 3 minutes, stirring, until fragrant and slightly softened.

Stir in white wine and cook until evaporated. Stir in mirin, vinegar, sugar and water. Simmer for 5 minutes.

Pour chili mixture and green onions into food processor and puree until almost smooth. Stir in mint and salt.

Rub lamb with remaining 1 tbsp olive oil and season with salt and pepper. Cook lamb in non-stick skillet on medium heat for 5 to 7 minutes per side for medium-rare. Let stand for 5 minutes. Cut across grain into ½-inch slices. Serve lamb with sauce.

Makes 4 servings.

RODNEY'S OYSTER HOUSE

[RODNEY CLARK AND ANN-MARIE CELESTINE]

Ask Rodney Clark to name his favourite oyster and he'll say Malpeque. Ask him when a Malpeque is at its best and he'll say, "When you're standing hip-deep in water in a bay off Prince Edward Island, and you reach down and pull one out and you open it. A cold pale ale to wash it down. Now that's a big moment for me. I'd say it doesn't get much better than that." For well over a decade, Rodney has been Toronto's (many would say Canada's) premier oyster man. Irredeemably sociable, he hosts the nightly party down in his Oyster House on Adelaide East, proving his point time and again that beer and oysters and laughter were made for each other. To hear him talk about Toronto's great nineteenth-century oyster presentation at the Turkish Coffee and Oyster Depot at Front and Church, you would swear he had been there. No wonder the crowd is so big around his portable ice boat at Taste. Tell us another one, Rodney...

WINE SUGGESTIONS
Canadian Chardonnay ❧
Chilean Chardonnay or Chilean Sauvignon Blanc
A gutsy quaffing white with good acidity and ample fruit to stand up to the tartare sauce.

CLARIFIED BUTTER

Clarified butter has had the milk solids removed, so it does not burn as easily when cooked at high temperatures. It also keeps longer than regular butter.

Place unsalted butter in saucepan on medium-low heat. Bring to simmer for 5 minutes or until solids separate. Cool slightly, then strain, discarding white liquid.

Miminegash Clam Burgers with Tartare Sauce

Serve tiny clam burgers on mini pitas for a great hors d'oeuvre or larger ones for a main course. Have the fishmonger shuck the clams for you. Substitute a pound of shrimp for the clams, if desired.

TARTARE SAUCE:
1 cup mayonnaise
1 tbsp finely chopped fresh parsley
1 tbsp finely chopped sweet pickle
1 tbsp chopped green olives
1 tbsp lemon juice
2 tsp finely chopped capers
1 tsp finely chopped shallots
1 tsp Dijon mustard
½ tsp hot red pepper sauce

CLAM BURGERS:
24 Cherrystone clams (quahogs), shucked
    and finely chopped
½ cup diced sweet red pepper

½ cup diced sweet green pepper
6 green onions, chopped
⅓ cup finely chopped fresh parsley
1 cup fine dry breadcrumbs
1 tbsp hot red pepper sauce
Salt and freshly ground pepper to taste
4 eggs, separated
2 tbsp vegetable oil
4 tsp clarified butter (page 120)

6 thick pita breads
1 tbsp olive oil
1 tomato, sliced thickly
Alfalfa sprouts

Stir together mayonnaise, 1 tbsp parsley, pickle, olives, lemon juice, capers, shallots, mustard and ½ tsp hot pepper sauce in small bowl.

Combine clams, sweet peppers, green onions, ⅓ cup parsley and breadcrumbs in large bowl. Stir in 1 tbsp hot pepper sauce, salt, pepper and egg yolks.

Beat egg whites in a separate bowl until soft peaks form. Gently fold into clam mixture. With wet hands, form mixture into 6 patties about ½ inch thick.

Heat vegetable oil and clarified butter in large non-stick skillet on medium heat. Cook burgers for 5 minutes, gently turning once, until nicely browned and cooked through.

Brush pitas with olive oil. Lightly grill for 30 seconds per side on barbecue or grill. Cut pitas in half and arrange burgers on pita halves. Layer tomato, tartare sauce and alfalfa sprouts on top of burgers. Top with remaining pita.

Makes 6 servings.

LE ROYAL MERIDIEN KING EDWARD HOTEL

[JOHN HIGGINS]

When John Higgins was learning to cook at Motherwell Technical College in Scotland, he would often sit and listen to his teacher, Mr. Hogan, talk of the times he had cooked at Gleneagles Hotel in Perthshire, at Buckingham Palace and in North America. "I would think, If he can do it, I can do it, too," muses Higgins. "And I did—at all three places." These days Higgins is the teacher, taking great pride in training his apprentices at Le Royal Meridien King Edward Hotel, where he plays two leading roles as executive chef and food and beverage manager. He remains a consummate cook, forever winning culinary competitions, cooking for small parties at the chef's table in the hotel kitchen and creating wonderful menus for its signature restaurant, Chiaro's. This year he is co-captain of Canada's culinary Olympic team—one more form of expression, one more way to do what he most loves doing.

WINE SUGGESTIONS
BC Pinot Blanc or Ontario Aligoté ✺
white Burgundy (Chablis) or Alsace Riesling
*Lemon, lime, chicken and raw tuna! This dish cries out for a white wine
with good acidity.*

Citrus Chicken with Pacific Tuna Tartare and Tobiko Drizzle

citrus chicken

A superb combination of flavours and textures makes this an exciting dish. Serve with jasmine rice and stir-fried asparagus.

CITRUS CHICKEN:
3 finely chopped cloves garlic
2 tsp finely chopped lemongrass
1 tbsp grated lemon rind
1 tbsp grated lime rind
1 tbsp grated orange rind
¼ cup olive oil
1 tbsp chopped fresh parsley
2 tsp chopped fresh tarragon
Salt and freshly ground pepper to taste
4 bone-in chicken breasts

TUNA TARTARE:
5 oz raw sushi-quality tuna
1 tbsp olive oil
2 tsp chopped fresh chives
1 tsp lemon juice
Salt and freshly ground pepper to taste

TOBIKO DRIZZLE:
2 tbsp rice vinegar
1 egg yolk
½ cup vegetable oil
1 tbsp flying fish roe (tobiko)
Salt, freshly ground pepper and lemon juice to taste

Whisk together garlic, lemongrass, lemon, lime and orange rinds, ¼ cup olive oil, parsley, tarragon, salt and pepper.

Place chicken in shallow dish and cover with marinade. Cover and refrigerate for 1 hour.

Preheat oven to 350°F. Drain chicken and reserve marinade.

Heat non-stick skillet on high heat. Sear chicken on both sides, about 2 minutes per side. Transfer to roasting pan. Roast in oven, basting often with marinade, for 30 to 40 minutes or until juices run clear. Do not baste for last 10 minutes of cooking time.

Chop tuna with sharp knife or in food processor. Stir in 1 tbsp olive oil, chives, lemon juice, salt and pepper.

Beat vinegar and egg yolk with whisk or hand blender. Slowly whisk in vegetable oil. Stir in fish roe and season with salt, pepper and lemon juice.

Serve chicken topped with tuna and drizzle with dressing.

Makes 4 servings

SENATOR RESTAURANT [FRANK SCORDINO]

This year, the Senator turns seventy-one—an extraordinary age for a Toronto restaurant—and the future has never looked more rosy, with the Yonge and Dundas development rejuvenating the neighbourhood. Bob Sniderman had long been a regular customer at the Senator diner when he heard, one morning in 1984, that the place was scheduled for demolition. He bought it and then set about the delicate task of turning it into a critically acclaimed restaurant without disturbing its classic diner charm. Five years later he added the more formal steakhouse next door, then the upstairs jazz club and lounge bar. On its quiet backstreet behind the Pantages theatre, the Senator grew, still a beloved institution but on a greater, more versatile scale. Now the city is opening up around it and Bob Sniderman, chef Frank Scordino and his team are making new plans for the diner, the healthiest, most attractive septuagenarian in town.

VIDALIA ONIONS

Vidalia onions are grown in Georgia. They are so sweet it is said you can eat them like an apple. They are in season from April to fall. Other sweet onions or Spanish onions may be substituted.

WINE SUGGESTIONS
Canadian Pinot Noir 🍁
red Bordeaux or a named Beaujolais village
A fruity red wine with lively acidity to stand up to the relish.

Grilled Sirloin Steak on Potato Bread with Grilled Vidalia Onion Relish

grilled vidalia

If you wish, you can use a thick 2-lb sirloin. You can also serve the steak without the bread and with the relish on top. Accompany with a tomato salad and French fries (page 23).

GRILLED VIDALIA ONION RELISH:
2 large Vidalia onions, cut in slices ½ inch thick
2 tbsp olive oil
1 tsp fennel seeds
1 tsp dried thyme

1 tbsp red wine vinegar
Salt and freshly ground pepper to taste

1 focaccia or potato baguette
4 8-oz New York steaks

Brush onion slices with a little oil and grill over medium-high heat until tender and brown, about 6 minutes per side. Dice and place in bowl.

Heat 1 tbsp olive oil in skillet over medium-high heat. Add fennel seeds and cook just until fragrant, about 1 to 2 minutes. Add fennel to onions, along with remaining oil, thyme, vinegar, salt and pepper. Cover with plastic wrap and refrigerate for 12 to 24 hours.

Cut bread into four and slice each piece in half horizontally. Toast or grill on both sides.

Season steak with salt and pepper and brush with a little oil. Grill over medium-high heat until medium-rare, about 5 minutes per side. Slice thinly.

Place steak on bread. Top with relish and second slice of bread.

Makes 4 servings.

SPLENDIDO

[ARPI MAGYAR]

BULGUR

Bulgur is wheat berries that have been steamed, dried and milled. Unlike other wheat berries, they only need to be soaked before using. Bulgur is used in salads such as tabbouleh.

Seated at the bar are two University of Toronto professors on a night out in the Annex, a food writer from the States eating incognito, a famous actor and his small but attentive entourage. The same sort of mix pertains in the beautiful dining room beyond — people who love the sociability of the room, or the looks, or the flattering lighting, but especially the food. Chef-owner Arpi Magyar, once of Pronto, then of Auberge du Pommier, for a while with Cucina, is as adept at making every guest feel welcome as he is at cooking. Try his slow-cooked osso buco, his rabbit terrine, his heavenly scallops, or this lamb sausage, if you should be lucky enough to find it on his seasonal menu.

WINE SUGGESTIONS
Canadian Cabernet Sauvignon
red Bordeaux or red Rioja (Spain)
Lots of spice here so Cabernet Sauvignon's your pick, unless you want to try a Tempranillo.

Grilled Lamb Sausages with Parsley Herb Salad

The savoury lamb mixture can also be formed into patties and grilled on the barbecue.

PARSLEY HERB SALAD:
1 cup bulgur
2 cups boiling water
½ cup chopped fresh parsley
½ cup chopped fresh mint
4 cups chopped Romaine lettuce
1 cup chopped red onion
1½ cups peeled, seeded and diced tomato
2 cups chopped green onions
⅓ cup olive oil
¼ cup lemon juice
Salt and freshly ground pepper to taste

LAMB SAUSAGES:
2 tbsp olive oil
1½ cups finely chopped onion
3 tbsp finely chopped garlic
3 tbsp chopped fresh rosemary or 1 tbsp dried
1 tbsp cumin seeds
1 tbsp fennel seeds
1 tsp hot red pepper flakes
2 lb ground lamb
½ tsp salt
¼ tsp cracked black peppercorns
Sausage casings

Combine bulgur and boiling water in large bowl. Cover and let stand for 15 minutes or until grain is tender and liquid absorbed. If there is any excess liquid, drain off. Cool.

Stir parsley, mint and lettuce into cooled bulgur. Gently fold in red onion, tomato and green onions up to 30 minutes before serving.

Whisk together ⅓ cup oil, lemon juice, salt and pepper in small bowl. Toss salad with dressing.

Heat 2 tbsp oil in skillet on medium heat. Cook onion for 4 to 5 minutes until soft and transparent. Add garlic and cook for 2 to 3 minutes until fragrant and softened.

Stir in rosemary, cumin, fennel seeds and hot pepper flakes. Remove from heat and let cool to room temperature.

Combine lamb with onion mixture in large bowl. Stir in salt and pepper. Cook small amount of mixture over medium-high heat in non-stick skillet until no longer pink; taste and add more seasonings if necessary. Fill sausage casings with lamb mixture.

Grill sausages for about 5 minutes per side or until slightly pink in centre. Serve with parsley and herb salad.

Makes 4 servings.

BONNIE STERN

Maybe you know Bonnie Stern from her weekly television show on WTN, or perhaps from the eight very successful cookbooks she has written. Or maybe you've attended some of the fascinating classes she has taught or hosted at the cooking school she started in 1973 on Erskine Avenue. Whatever the connection, it is extremely unlikely that anyone interested in Toronto's food scene is unaware of Bonnie and her many achievements. Among them is her role as one of the pioneering co-chairs (with Kathryn Rayczak and Lisa Slater) of the first ever Taste, in 1991. "It was quite an adventure," she remembers. "We had more than thirty chefs, and the wineries—nothing had ever been done on that kind of scale—and we held the event at the top of the CN Tower. Somehow we organized the whole thing in six weeks and it worked like magic!" Bonnie chose this recipe for chicken tagine because it is easy to make ahead, but also delectably exotic.

WINE SUGGESTIONS
Canadian off-dry Riesling 🍁
Rheingau Riesling Spätlese
The rich spicing of this dish calls for an aromatic white wine with some residual sugar.

Chicken Tagine with Honeyed Tomatoes and Couscous

A tagine is a Moroccan cooking vessel made of clay. It has a deep round dish and a triangular, funnel-shaped top and is used for both cooking and serving. This delicious low-fat spiced chicken dish is suitable for entertaining.

1 tbsp olive oil
8 bone-in chicken breasts, skin removed
Salt and freshly ground pepper to taste
1 onion, finely chopped
3 cloves garlic, finely chopped
1 tbsp grated ginger
1 tsp ground cumin
1 tsp ground cinnamon
¼ tsp cayenne

½ tsp saffron threads, crushed and dissolved
   in 2 tbsp boiling water
1 28-oz/796 mL can plum tomatoes, crushed
   with juices
3 tbsp honey
1 tbsp lemon juice
3 cups Israeli couscous
1 tbsp toasted sesame seeds
¼ cup chopped fresh coriander

Heat oil in large, deep non-stick skillet on high heat.

Season chicken with salt and pepper. Brown well on both sides. Remove chicken from skillet and discard all but 1 tsp oil from pan.

Reduce heat to medium and add onion, garlic and ginger to skillet. Cook gently for a few minutes until tender. Add cumin, cinnamon and cayenne. Cook for 30 seconds. Add saffron water, tomatoes and honey and bring to boil.

Return chicken to pan. Cover and simmer gently for 20 minutes or just until chicken is cooked.

Remove chicken from pan and keep warm.

Add lemon juice to sauce and bring to boil. If sauce is not thick enough, boil, uncovered, until reduced. Combine sauce with chicken.

Cook Israeli couscous in a large pot of boiling water until cooked, about 5 minutes. (If you are using regular couscous, follow package directions.) Place in large serving bowl and pour chicken and sauce on top. Sprinkle with sesame seeds and coriander.

Makes 8 servings.

TERRA

[Raffaello Ferrari]

Thornhill became terra cognita to Toronto's gastronomes when Franco Prevedello opened this beautiful restaurant in 1993. Today it belongs to Mark McEwan—a smooth fine-dining operation for those who eat out north of the city, but this recipe dates from its early days when Raffaello Ferrari was chef. Charming, much loved and brilliantly gifted both in the kitchen and in the dining room, Ferrari burst onto Toronto's scene in 1980 as chef of Biffi Bistro and Pronto, Prevedello's first revolutionary restaurants. It was the dawn of Cal-Ital cooking, and Raffaello quickly established himself as high priest of the cuisine, endlessly imitated but never surpassed. When Prevedello opened Centro, Ferrarri was there as well, eventually moving on to Orso, where he cooked more brilliantly than ever, to Tutto Bene and finally Terra. He died tragically early at the age of forty-one.

Wine Suggestions
Canadian Merlot ❧
Amarone (Veneto) or Tuscan Sangiovese
An earthy red wine with lots of fruit extract, preferably Italian.

Tortellini with Mushroom Cream Sauce

This can also be served as a first course or as a side dish with grilled veal. You could also include some wild mushrooms in the mixture. Shave the Parmesan over the tortellini for a pretty presentation.

3 tbsp butter
2 tbsp olive oil
2 tbsp chopped onion
1½ lb mushrooms, sliced
½ cup whipping cream
2 tbsp brandy

2 tsp lemon juice
Salt and freshly ground pepper to taste
1 lb cooked cheese-stuffed tortellini or ravioli
½ cup grated or shaved Parmesan cheese
Fresh rosemary sprigs

Heat butter and oil in large skillet on medium heat. Add onion and cook, stirring, for 3 to 5 minutes or until softened. Add mushrooms and cook for 6 to 8 minutes, stirring frequently, until half the moisture has evaporated.

Stir in cream, brandy, lemon juice, salt and pepper. Simmer over medium heat, stirring frequently, until cream has reduced by half, about 15 minutes.

Add cooked pasta and toss to coat well. Sprinkle with cheese and garnish with rosemary.

Makes 4 servings.

LUCY WAVERMAN

You think you're busy? Try keeping up with Lucy Waverman. Cordon Bleu trained, with an Ontario Teacher's Certificate and a degree in journalism, she owned and directed The Cooking School for eighteen years. She has her own weekly cooking show on City TV's CityLine, writes a weekly food column for the *Globe and Mail* and is food consultant to the Liquor Control Board of Ontario. Her recipes are the heart and soul of the LCBO magazine, *Food & Drink*, she has published eight books of her own and contributed to umpteen others, and she's a frequent guest on radio and TV shows, in demand whenever culinary expertise is called for. She also sits on the boards of several organizations, including Second Harvest. But for those who are lucky enough to work with Lucy, such credentials come second to her unfailing enthusiasm, her wisdom and the generosity with which she shares her time, her knowledge and her ideas. Professional cooks are guided by her opinions; her readers know they can follow her recipes with total confidence.

WINE SUGGESTIONS
Ontario Gamay Noir ❧
Beaujolais-Villages or the named crus of
Beaujolais (Fleurie, Morgon, etc.)
With dark meat I prefer a light red wine, but you could go with a white
(Sauvignon Blanc or Chardonnay).

Ballotine of Chicken with Spinach and Crisped Vegetables

A simple, well-flavoured dish. Traditionally, a ballotine referred to cold stuffed fish, chicken or meat served beautifully garnished as the centrepiece of a magnificent buffet. Today the term ballotine means a stuffed leg of any kind of poultry, served hot from the oven. Ask the butcher to bone out the thighs for you.

Make the crisped vegetables and spinach ahead of time and reheat in the oven. Garlic mashed potatoes make a heavenly side dish.

¼ cup chopped fresh parsley
1 tbsp chopped fresh thyme
1 tsp grated lemon rind
2 tbsp butter, at room temperature
Salt and freshly ground pepper to taste
4 chicken legs, thigh bones removed
1 tbsp olive oil
2 tbsp butter

2 bunches spinach, cleaned and steamed
1 tbsp lemon juice

CRISPED VEGETABLES:
Vegetable oil
1 sweet potato, peeled and shredded
2 parsnips, peeled and shredded

Preheat oven to 400°F.

Combine parsley, thyme, lemon rind, 2 tbsp butter, salt and pepper in small bowl. Fill cavities in chicken legs left from removed thigh bones. Fold skin over and fasten with toothpicks.

Heat olive oil in non-stick skillet on medium heat. Add chicken skin side down and cook for 3 minutes or until browned. Turn chicken and cook second side for 3 minutes.

Place chicken in baking dish and bake for 25 to 30 minutes or until juices are clear. Pour off any juices. Skim fat and reserve juices.

Heat 2 tbsp butter in skillet on medium heat and add spinach. Cook until heated through, about 3 minutes, and stir in reserved juices from chicken. Season with lemon juice, salt and pepper.

Heat about ¼ inch oil in small skillet on medium-high heat. Sprinkle in vegetables a handful at a time and cook until crisp, about 30 seconds. Remove with slotted spoon.

Serve chicken on bed of spinach and top with crisped vegetables.

Makes 4 servings.

WINDSOR ARMS [JEAN-PIERRE CHALLET]

The phoenix has risen from the ashes. The legendary Windsor Arms has been rebuilt, with every exterior brick meticulously replaced and a brand-new Courtyard Café to serve as the next generation's arena of dreams and celebrations. Years in the making, the restaurant is the domain of Executive Chef J-P Challet, once of the Inn at Manitou and Auberge du Pommier. With Paul Drake back on the piano (the past twenty years vanish as he plays), it seems appropriate that parts of J-P's menu refer to the classics such as moules marinières and chateaubriand for two, but also to the more contemporary, creative side of his repertoire—a trio of foie gras recipes on a single plate, an agnolotti stuffed with smoked salmon as garnish for a cloudlike fillet of cod. To understand his ways more deeply you can watch him in action at the chef's table in his kitchen, or else work with this recipe in yours.

WINE SUGGESTIONS
BC Pinot Gris or Ontario unoaked Chardonnay ✺
Alsace Tokay-Pinot Gris
The saltiness and piquancy of the sauce suggest a white wine with good fruit and fresh acidity.

Pickerel Mille-Feuille with Honey Mushrooms and Tartare Sauce Emulsion

Emulsions are very fashionable. To make them, use a hand blender or frother to give a cappuccino-like look to sauces and soups. If you can't find honey mushrooms, use shiitakes or chanterelles.

1 egg yolk
½ tsp Dijon mustard
¾ cup grapeseed oil
1 tbsp lemon juice
3 tbsp finely chopped gherkins or sweet pickle
2 tbsp small capers
1 tbsp finely chopped shallots
1 tbsp finely chopped fresh parsley
Hot red pepper sauce, salt and freshly ground
   pepper to taste

3 8-inch square spring roll wrappers
3 tbsp olive oil
8 oz honey mushrooms
¼ cup finely chopped shallots
1 clove garlic, finely chopped
4 pickerel fillets (about 6 oz each)
¼ cup water
2 tbsp chopped fresh thyme

Whisk egg yolk with mustard in small bowl. Gradually whisk in grapeseed oil until thick and smooth. Stir in lemon juice, gherkins, capers, 1 tbsp shallots and parsley. Season with hot pepper sauce, salt and pepper. Refrigerate.

Preheat oven to 375°F. Cut each spring roll wrapper into 4 triangles and arrange on lightly oiled baking sheet. Brush with 1 tbsp olive oil and bake for 5 minutes or until golden.

Heat 1 tbsp olive oil in large skillet over medium-high heat. Cook mushrooms, ¼ cup shallots and garlic for 4 minutes, stirring until tender. Season with salt and pepper. Keep warm.

Cut each fish fillet into four pieces. Heat remaining 1 tbsp olive oil in large skillet over medium-high heat. In batches, cook fish for 2 to 3 minutes per side or until golden on outside and cooked through. (Add more oil to pan if needed.) Sprinkle cooked fish with salt and pepper.

Bring ¼ cup water to boil in small saucepan. Remove from heat. Add gherkin sauce and blend.

Place spring roll triangle in centre of each of four dinner plates. Distribute half of mushroom mixture on top of triangles. Layer each with two pieces of fish, a spring roll triangle, 2 more pieces of fish and a third triangle. Divide remaining mushrooms among plates and drizzle sauce around mille-feuilles. Sprinkle with thyme and serve immediately.

Makes 4 servings.

XANGÔ

[TREVOR BERRYMAN]

Odd to think how exotic Latin fine dining seemed only four years ago, when Trevor Berryman opened Xangô. Suddenly there was a whole new vocabulary of ingredients to learn, new flavours and textures that puzzled and amazed restaurant-goers raised within Franco-Italian traditions. Berryman himself had been introduced to the culture only a couple of years earlier when he opened a dance club called Babalu with a Colombian partner, Nubia Solano. But Xangô was and is the real thing, with menus devised by Douglas Rodriguez from Patria in New York, now lovingly interpreted by chef Gustavo Agreda. Subtle and subtly different, the cooking has been a revelation for Toronto, and so has the dancing that erupts on the ground floor every Saturday night — salsa, cumbia, muchada, merengue. Life is good in the Latin quarter.

WINE SUGGESTIONS
Canadian dry Riesling
Alsace Riesling or Tokay-Pinot Gris
The mojo sauce with its citric tartness requires a very dry
white wine with good acidity.

Fresh Chilean Sea Bass with Calamari Rice and Cuban Mojo

The bright flavours and fresh taste of this Cuban-influenced dish make an intriguing main course.
Mojo is a fresh-tasting Cuban sauce that can be served over grilled chicken, steaks and pork.
If squid ink is not available, use an extra ¼ cup stock.

CALAMARI RICE:
3 tbsp olive oil
3 tbsp diced Spanish onion
3 tbsp diced sweet red peppers
3 tbsp diced sweet yellow peppers
2 cloves garlic, finely chopped
1 tsp ground cumin
2 bay leaves
2 cups lobster or fish stock
4 oz fresh calamari rings and tentacles
2 cups long-grain rice
¼ cup calamari ink

CUBAN MOJO:
2 tbsp chopped fresh parsley
2 tbsp chopped fresh oregano
2 tbsp chopped garlic
2 tbsp chopped toasted almonds
Salt to taste
½ cup lime juice
½ cup olive oil

4 pieces Chilean sea bass (about 6 oz each)
2 tsp olive oil
Salt and freshly ground pepper to taste

Preheat oven to 300°F.

Heat 3 tbsp oil in large ovenproof skillet over medium-high heat. Add onion and peppers. Cook, stirring, for 3 minutes. Add finely chopped garlic, cumin, bay leaves, stock and calamari. Bring just to boil.

Add rice. Reduce heat to low and simmer for about 10 minutes or until most of stock is absorbed. Stir in calamari ink. Cover and bake for about 25 minutes or until rice is tender and all of liquid has been absorbed. Remove bay leaves.

Blend parsley, oregano, chopped garlic, almonds, salt and lime juice in food processor or blender until chunky. With machine running, slowly add ½ cup olive oil.

Brush sea bass lightly with 2 tsp olive oil, salt and pepper. Grill over medium-high heat just until cooked through and opaque, about 5 to 6 minutes per side.

Serve fish with calamari rice and drizzle with mojo.

Makes 4 servings.

Desserts

ALL THE BEST FINE FOODS

[JANE RODMELL AND SUE BOWMAN]

TOASTING NUTS

Spread shelled nuts on a baking sheet and bake at 350°F for 8 to 10 minutes or until golden.

It started with an idea that occurred to Jane Rodmell in 1984: open a store that would gather the city's best breads in one convenient location. Today, All the Best is one of Toronto's handful of truly accomplished gourmet food stores, still bringing in breads from other fine bakeries but also selling its own fabulous loaves made on the premises by David Moore. And the business has grown to encompass a world of party supplies, wonderful cakes and biscuits, scrumptious prepared foods, cherished cheeses and a dazzling inventory of treats, many of them made by the artisanal Canadian companies that Rodmell delights in discovering. From the beginning she has welcomed the arrival of Second Harvest's van two or three times a week, happy to lend her support to such a logical, generous cause. In some ways it's just another aspect of her original idea—another way to share the city's and her store's resources —all of the best, and nothing but.

WINE SUGGESTIONS
Canadian Late Harvest Riesling 🍁
Tuscan Vin Santo
Go Italian. Dunk your biscotti in a glass of chilled dessert wine, preferably Vin Santo.

Almond and Hazelnut Biscotti

almond and hazelnut

These are traditional rustic-looking biscotti, perfect for dunking into coffee. If you allow them to sit for three days before eating, the lemon flavour will become more pronounced. Store in an airtight container for up to one month or freeze for up to three months.

---

5 eggs
2 cups granulated sugar
½ cup butter, melted
2 tbsp grated lemon rind
1½ cups toasted whole blanched almonds

4 cups all-purpose flour
½ cup toasted ground hazelnuts
2 tsp baking powder
1 tsp cinnamon

Preheat oven to 350°F. Line 2 baking sheets with parchment paper.

Whisk eggs in large bowl until frothy. Whisk in sugar, melted butter and lemon rind.

Chop ½ cup almonds coarsely. In separate large bowl, combine chopped almonds with remaining 1 cup whole almonds, flour, hazelnuts, baking powder and cinnamon.

Stir flour mixture into egg mixture one-third at a time until dough is formed. With floured hands, form dough into four 12 x 2½-inch logs. Smooth tops and sides and transfer to baking sheets.

Bake for about 30 minutes or until firm; rotate pans once during baking. Cool slightly.

Cut warm logs into diagonal slices ½ inch thick. Return slices to baking sheet cut side down.

Bake for another 20 minutes or until crisp and golden; rotate pans once during baking time.

Makes about 3 dozen biscotti.

BAKER STREET BAKERY

[MARY SOMERTON AND ESTHER KRAVICE]

Mary Somerton and Esther Kravice have moved their business several times since 1978, the year they founded Baker Street. It all began in their own kitchens, progressed to a mid-city bakery and now to a large and busy warehouse, from where they supply a host of restaurants, hotels and caterers. Through it all, they have never wavered in their commitment to producing irresistible desserts like this Skor™ chocolate cake. "There is such a demand for anything with caramel or butterscotch," says Esther. "These are the flavours of the new millennium!"

VANILLA BEANS

Vanilla beans have a depth of flavour and an aromatic sweetness that vanilla extract lacks. Store the beans in a cupboard. After you have used them, rinse and dry and then bury in a jar of sugar. Use the flavoured sugar in coffee, cookies and cakes.

WINE SUGGESTIONS

Canadian "port" style fortified wine ☀
Samos Muscat (Greece) or California Orange Muscat
Something really sweet is called for. Orange-flavoured fortified wines or liqueurs make a great counterpoint of flavours.

Skor™ Bar Cake

You can omit the Skor™ bars or use other chocolate bars in this extra-rich cake.

BROWNIE CAKE:
12 oz semisweet chocolate, chopped
1 cup butter
1 cup granulated sugar
3 eggs
1 tbsp vanilla
½ cup all-purpose flour
1 tsp baking powder

MOUSSE FILLING:
1 cup chocolate milk
1 vanilla bean, split, or 1 tsp vanilla
1 lb semisweet chocolate, chopped
¾ cup whipping cream
1 cup crumbled Skor™ bars (about 4 bars)

Preheat oven to 300°F. Oil a 13 x 9-inch baking dish and line bottom with parchment paper.

Melt 12 oz chocolate and butter in heavy saucepan on low heat, stirring occasionally.

Beat sugar, eggs and vanilla in large bowl with electric beaters on medium speed for 2 minutes. Scrape down sides of bowl and beat for 2 minutes longer or until light and fluffy.

Stir in melted chocolate mixture and beat until combined. Add flour and baking powder. Beat on low speed for 1 minute. Pour into prepared pan.

Bake for 22 to 25 minutes or until cake is set but not dry. Cool in pan on rack. Cake will be firm when chilled.

Combine chocolate milk with vanilla bean and 1 lb chocolate in a heavy saucepan on low heat. Stir together until chocolate is melted, about 5 minutes. Remove from heat and cool. Remove vanilla bean.

Whip cream in bowl until stiff peaks form and fold into cooled chocolate mixture. Refrigerate for 30 minutes or until spreadable.

Invert brownie cake onto baking sheet and cut in half horizontally. Spread half of mousse filling on one half of cake. Sprinkle with half the crumbled Skor™ bars. Repeat layers. Chill until ready to serve. Cut into small squares.

Makes 8 to 10 servings.

DAWN ADRIENNE BERNEY

Dawn Adrienne Berney's extraordinarily busy career began in Paris in 1984, when she enrolled in the Cordon Bleu cooking school to study cooking and pastry. After several restaurant internships and a stint as pastry chef at Chez Julien, she worked for a year as executive chef for the U.S. Consulate General in Paris before setting off to travel through Asia. She finally returned to Canada in 1989 and soon opened her own full-time catering company with a second business making chocolate truffles. She was Bonnie Stern's right hand during the first ever Taste '91 and was her co-chair the following year. She chaired the event herself in 1993 and 1994. As if all this didn't give her enough to do, she also began food styling for feature films, an aspect of her work that she still finds enormously satisfying. "But my catering company remains my mainstay and passion," she says. "My specialty is fresh market cuisine—simple and healthy, with French and Asian influences from my travels. And, of course, I do all our desserts."

WINE SUGGESTIONS
Canadian off-dry sparkling wine 🍁
Demi Sec champagne
The most decadent of chocolate deserves the most decadent of wines—
an off-dry sparkler.

Chocolate Truffles

These are the best truffles ever. You could make them half the size and still satisfy the most intense chocolate craving. Use a good-quality bittersweet chocolate such as Valrhona or Callebaut. The truffles can be flavoured with a few tablespoons of liqueur or Champagne; add it along with the whipping cream. They can also be dusted with icing sugar or chocolate sprinkles instead of cocoa.

1¼ lb bittersweet or semisweet chocolate
1 cup butter

½ cup whipping cream
1 cup cocoa, sifted

Melt 8 oz chocolate with butter in top of double boiler over hot water. Cool to room temperature.

Whip cream in bowl until it holds its shape. Fold into chocolate mixture.

Pipe or spoon by tablespoon (about 30 blobs) onto baking sheet lined with parchment paper. Refrigerate until firm enough to handle.

Shape chocolate into balls with cool hands. Refrigerate again until firm.

Melt remaining 12 oz chocolate and let cool to room temperature.

Place cocoa in large shallow dish.

Dip each truffle into melted chocolate. Place truffles in dish of cocoa and refrigerate until cold. Shake pan to dust truffles with cocoa. Store in covered container.

Makes about 30 truffles.

LORENE SAURO

FRUIT SAUCE

In a small saucepan, combine cooled leftover fruit syrup with 1½ tsp cornstarch and bring to a boil. Serve sauce with the triangles or with pancakes.

It was the unsatisfying flavour of the cakes she bought that first started Lorene Sauro thinking perhaps she could do it better. She began to bake, encouraged by friends and relatives and then by a trickle of orders from strangers who had heard of her talents. The next step was to cook for a tearoom up in Aurora, and then for Fitz-Henri Fine Foods down in Toronto. In 1985, after taking a course of Cordon Bleu cooking classes with Beverley Burge, she rented her own kitchen space in Woodbridge and formed her own company, Beyond Words. Using the finest ingredients—organic wherever possible—she developed a line of forty cakes and desserts, supplying top gourmet stores with the likes of raspberry chocolate ganache, triple orange liqueur cake and cappuccino mousse—all of them handmade. "What other way is there?" says Lorene.

WINE SUGGESTIONS
Ontario Framboise 🍁
Ruby Port
A sweet, fortified fruit wine or an inexpensive port will do the trick nicely.

Chocolate Velvet Triangles with Fruit and Cream

An elegant, luscious dessert with a rich chocolate flavour and fresh berries for contrast. Serve with a dollop of whipped cream.

FRUIT COMPOTE:
½ cup water
½ cup granulated sugar
2 cups fresh berries
¼ cup fruit liqueur

CHOCOLATE SHORTBREAD CRUST:
1⅓ cups all-purpose flour
⅓ cup granulated sugar
⅔ cup cold butter, cubed

2 tbsp cocoa, sifted
2 oz semisweet chocolate, melted

CHOCOLATE CUSTARD:
2¼ cups whipping cream
5 oz semisweet chocolate, melted
½ cup granulated sugar
3 eggs
½ tsp vanilla

Preheat oven to 350°F. Line 8-inch square cake pan with foil, leaving 2-inch overhang on two sides to use as handles.

Combine water and ½ cup sugar in saucepan and bring to boil. Boil for 2 minutes or until syrup starts to thicken slightly. Gently stir in fruit and liqueur; cook for 1 minute. Remove from heat and let cool. Drain compote in fine sieve (use leftover syrup to make fruit sauce, page 146).

Place flour, ⅓ cup sugar, butter and cocoa in food processor. Process to fine crumbs.

Press crumbs firmly into prepared pan. Bake for 20 to 30 minutes or until set. Brush top with 2 oz melted chocolate; cool.

Warm whipping cream in saucepan and remove from heat. Whisk in 5 oz melted chocolate, ½ cup sugar, eggs and vanilla until completely smooth.

Spread strained fruit over shortbread; pour custard over top. Bake for 50 to 60 minutes or until custard is puffed and set at edges but still a bit loose in centre. Cool in pan on rack.

Cover with plastic wrap and refrigerate for about 6 hours or until completely cold. Run a hot, dry knife around edge of pan and lift entire piece carefully from the pan. Trim edges. Cut into 6 rectangles and cut each rectangle into 2 triangles.

Makes 12 triangles.

BROWNES BISTRO

[BEVERLEY BURGE]

Beverley Burge's recipe for Brownes Brownies has come a long way. "I got it from my mother," she says. "I spent my life cooking when I was a kid. Baking was my thing. Though we would have used walnuts not pecans in New Zealand." Burge had already been a Cordon Bleu instructor in England when she moved to Toronto in 1980. For the next seven years, she ran her own cooking school before opening Brownes Bistro. It remains Rosedale's beloved neighbourhood spot, as famous for sausage and mash as for crème brûlée. "We still take it one day at a time," says Beverley, "and every minute's exciting."

WINE SUGGESTIONS
The best match for this dessert is a glass of milk—a dessert made for sharing!

CHOCOLATE

Unsweetened chocolate contains no sugar and is used in recipes where a dense, bitter chocolate taste is needed. *Bittersweet chocolate* has some sugar added and has a concentrated chocolate flavour. *Semisweet chocolate* contains even more sugar, though it can be used as a substitute for bittersweet. *Milk chocolate* contains milk solids; only use it in cooking when a recipe specifically calls for it.

Brownes Brownies

brownies

The famous brownie recipe. Very chocolatey and not too sweet—definitely an adult brownie. Dust with sifted icing sugar, if desired.

1 cup all-purpose flour
¾ cup cocoa
2 cups dark brown sugar
½ tsp salt
4 eggs

¾ cup butter, melted
2 tsp vanilla
2 cups chopped pecans
6 oz semisweet or bittersweet chocolate,
    coarsely chopped

Preheat oven to 350°F. Line 13 x 9-inch cake pan with parchment paper.

Sift flour with cocoa into large bowl. Stir in brown sugar and salt.

Whisk together eggs, melted butter and vanilla in separate bowl. Stir into dry ingredients until moistened. Stir in pecans and chocolate. Pour into prepared pan, spreading evenly with spatula.

Bake for about 30 minutes or until top is firm to touch and cake tester comes out clean. Cool in pan on rack for at least 10 minutes before cutting into squares. Serve warm or cool.

Makes 15 to 20 squares.

DUFFLET PASTRIES [DUFFLET ROSENBERG]

It seems incredible that more than twenty years have passed since Dufflet Rosenberg sold her first cake to the Cow Café, a cake she had baked in her mother's kitchen. From that small beginning she has used her talent, imagination and business acumen to build a city-wide empire of deliciously fresh pastries, cakes and desserts. How many restaurants, lacking a pastry chef, have passed off her white chocolate mousse cake as their own? How many harried hostesses have lifted one of her pies off its telltale black-and-white spiral base and made the same claim? New treats are constantly added to her formidable repertoire, tempting customers into her retail café on Queen Street West. Halloween wouldn't be Halloween without Dufflet's ghost-shaped butter cookies. Christmas wouldn't be Christmas without her cranberry orange cheesecake.

WINE SUGGESTIONS
Canadian Select Late Harvest Vidal 🍁
Sauternes (Bordeaux) or Samos Muscat (Greece)
You don't really need wine with these delicious pastries, but if you feel the urge
try a white dessert wine with lots of residual sweetness.

These Eastern European Jewish pastries are traditionally served at celebrations, but they are so mouth-watering that they are a treat at any time of the year. The filling can be varied using your choice of nuts, dried fruits and jam.

- -

8 oz cream cheese, cubed
1 cup butter, cubed
2 cups all-purpose flour
¼ tsp salt
⅓ cup raspberry jam
½ cup granulated sugar

1 tsp cinnamon
1 cup finely chopped pecans
½ cup currants
1 egg yolk
1 tsp water

- -

Blend cream cheese and butter together in food processor or electric mixer until smooth. Gradually beat in flour and salt until dough forms.

Divide dough into 3 equal pieces. Cover with plastic wrap and refrigerate until firm, at least 4 hours.

Preheat oven to 350°F. Line 2 baking sheets with parchment paper.

Remove one piece of dough from refrigerator and allow to sit for 10 minutes to soften. Roll into 12-inch circle. Spread with thin layer of jam.

Combine sugar and cinnamon and sprinkle one-third of mixture over jam. Sprinkle with one-third of the nuts and currants. With rolling pin, gently press filling ingredients into dough.

Cut circle into 12 wedges using pizza cutter or knife. Roll each piece into crescent shape from outside edge to point. Place point down on baking sheets. Repeat with remaining dough and filling.

Stir egg yolk and water in small bowl just until mixed. Brush glaze over rugelach. Bake for 20 to 25 minutes or until golden brown. Cool on racks.

Makes 36 pastries.

EIGENSINN FARM

[MICHAEL AND NOBUYO STADTLÄNDER]

Cook, farmer, philosopher, guru, supporter of righteous causes—Michael Stadtländer has been a towering figure in the lives of Toronto gourmets since he came here in 1980 to share the kitchen with Jamie Kennedy at Scaramouche. He brought with him the precepts of European nouvelle cuisine, but it has been his unique interpretations of Canada's gastronomic potential that have made him so profoundly influential, first at Stadtländer's, then, gloriously, at Nekah and now at Eigensinn Farm. It really is a farm—a community—organic, singular, a work forever in progress where Michael and his wife, Nobuyo, offer extraordinary meals and hospitality to those who make the pilgrimage to Singhampton. Growing up in Germany, Michael Stadtländer dreamed of a Canada of wild places, bountiful and brimming with indigenous treasures. At Eigensinn he has found—or created—the spirit of such a place, and it is our great good fortune that he chooses to share it.

WINE SUGGESTIONS
Canadian sparkling wine Sec ❋
Demi-Sec champagne
To balance the tart nature of the lemon flavour, a refreshing glass of off-dry sparkling wine.

Lemon Foam with Wild Blueberry Preserves

This mousse has a fluffy texture and a lively, lemony flavour that is offset by the rich blueberry sauce. The recipe can be halved, if desired.

1 tbsp powdered gelatin	10 egg yolks
¼ cup cold water	2 cups whipping cream
⅓ cup grated lemon rind	7 egg whites
2 cups fresh lemon juice	¼ cup sour cream
1½ cups granulated sugar	3 cups wild blueberry preserves (page 152)

Stir together gelatin and cold water in small saucepan. Place on low heat and stir until gelatin has dissolved.

Whisk together lemon rind, lemon juice, 1 cup sugar and egg yolks in large metal bowl set over pot of hot (not boiling) water. Cook on medium-low heat, whisking often, for about 15 minutes until creamy and tripled in volume. Remove bowl from heat and whisk in gelatin. Let cool for about 30 minutes or until room temperature, stirring occasionally.

Whip whipping cream in bowl with electric beaters until stiff. In separate bowl and using clean beaters, beat egg whites until soft peaks form. Gradually add remaining ½ cup sugar, beating until stiff but not dry.

Whisk sour cream into lemon mixture. In three additions, fold in whipped cream. Again, in three additions, fold in beaten egg whites. Pour into large bowl, cover with plastic wrap and refrigerate for 12 to 24 hours. Spoon or pipe into individual serving dishes. Serve with blueberry preserves.

Makes about 16 servings.

FRED'S BREAD

[ANDREA DAMON GIBSON]

Working the early-morning shift in Splendido's kitchen for three and a half years, pastry chef Andrea Damon Gibson made a discovery. Much as she loved creating stunning desserts such as spiced quince compote or goat cheese caramel mousse, she loved baking the restaurant's breads even more. So she quit the business and opened a bakery of her own, Fred's Bread. Handmade, using organic flour, her gorgeous loaves are baked at a low temperature to give them a super-crunchy crust, and the recipes can be as inventive as any dessert. Over the years, she has given us loaves of sun-dried tomato with thyme, potato focaccia with Parmigiano Reggiano and chives, and fabulous pumpkin bread.

With its maple mascarpone cream, this recipe shows the delicious dividends that accrue when a baker has a past as a pastry chef.

WINE SUGGESTIONS
Canadian Late Harvest Riesling 🍁
Sauternes (Bordeaux) or Monbazillac (SW France)
A rich, white dessert wine with a suggestion of apple and spice on the palate.

LEFTOVER EGG WHITES

Leftover egg whites can be used in meringues, pavlovas, omelettes and frittatas. They can be refrigerated for up to 5 days or frozen in quantities of 3 or 4 until needed.

Toasted Apple Cinnamon Rounds with Maple Mascarpone Cream

This little treat makes a perfect nibble with afternoon tea. If an apple cinnamon baguette is un-available, use a raisin or muesli baguette sprinkled with a touch of cinnamon before toasting. Before serving, drizzle the rounds with extra maple syrup and chopped toasted walnuts if desired.

1 apple cinnamon baguette	2 tbsp granulated sugar
½ cup whipping cream	3 tbsp maple syrup
½ cup mascarpone cheese, at room temperature	3 tbsp dark rum
5 egg yolks	

Cut baguette into slices ½ inch thick. Place on baking sheet. Toast 6 inches below preheated broiler for 1 minute or until golden. Turn and toast other side.

Whip cream in bowl until soft peaks form. Add mascarpone and whip until smooth and thickened.

Whisk egg yolks and sugar in separate metal bowl. Whisk in maple syrup and rum. Place bowl over saucepan of simmering water and cook, whisking constantly, for about 6 minutes or until mixture is thick enough to hold a ribbon. Remove from heat and immediately scrape mixture into clean bowl. Whisk occasionally until completely cool.

Whisk mascarpone mixture a bit at a time into egg mixture, beating until completely smooth. Pipe or spoon 1 tbsp mascarpone cream onto each baguette slice.

Makes about 32 rounds.

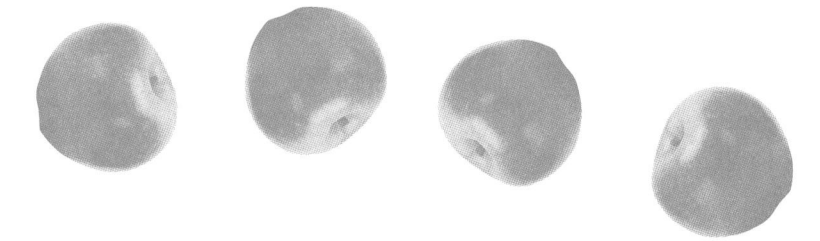

GELATO FRESCO

Sorbet is a frozen mixture of fruit and sugar with, occasionally, spirits added. It contains no cream, so is lighter than ice cream and much less fattening. The fruit should be fresh and more than ripe for the most intense flavour.

Sorbets are sometimes served between courses to refresh the palate.

Coming up with an exciting new recipe for Taste every year is an enjoyable challenge for Gelato Fresco's founder, Hart Melvin, especially since Inniskillin winery started providing him with Late Harvest wine as a special ingredient. The story of the company begins in the mid eighties, when Melvin was a regular customer at Pronto and often talked to Franco Prevedello and chef Raffaello Ferrari about the lack of terrific ice cream in Toronto. "They encouraged me to go to Milan," remembers Melvin, "and there I cashed in some serious karmic chips when I met my teacher, a man whose family had been making gelato for generations. When I came back, I started refining the recipes in my basement, then running round to Pronto with the ice creams and sorbets for Raffaello to use." Within a year, Gelato Fresco was being served at the Swiss and Ontario pavilions at Expo '86. "We went from nothing to real busy," adds Melvin—and Toronto has had terrific ice cream ever since.

WINE SUGGESTIONS
Canadian Select Harvest Riesling 🍁
Champagne Sec (France)
The wine you use to prepare the sorbet may not be sweet enough to match so take it up a notch—from Late Harvest to Select Late Harvest, or try an off-dry sparkling wine.

156 THE CHEF'S TABLE

Late Harvest Papaya Sorbet

An extraordinary sorbet to serve for dessert. Serve a small wafer or Coconut Tuile (page 169) on the side.

---

2 lb overripe papayas (about 3)
1 750 mL bottle Late Harvest Riesling

1 cup + 2 tbsp granulated sugar

Peel, seed and puree papayas. Place in large bowl and add wine and sugar, stirring until sugar is dissolved.

Freeze in ice-cream maker according to manufacturer's directions. Alternatively, pour into shallow metal tray, place in freezer, and stir every 30 to 40 minutes until thick. Blend in food processor to break up crystals. Cover and refreeze until firm.

Makes about 8 cups.

GRANO

Robert Martella and his wife, Lucia Ruggiero-Martella, live above the shop. A small point, perhaps, but it's one of the innumerable details that has always set Grano in a class of its own. The Martellas are there—Lucia down in the kitchen, keeping an eye on the next batch of bread, sending up dishes of tempting hot and cold antipasti to the long counter where customers make their selections; Robert, an avuncular presence by the central, horseshoe-shaped bar, greeting and taking orders, advising on wines, an oracle of Italian culture. When they opened their restaurant in the mid 1980s, customers loved the noise and bustle, the wild, paint-splashed decor, the unpretentious domesticity of it all. Since then, a dozen fads have come and gone but Grano remains the same—a little bigger now, but still as warm and genuine as the aroma of freshly baked bread.

WINE SUGGESTIONS
Canadian Riesling Icewine 🍁
Recioto di Soave (Veneto) or Pedro Ximenez Sherry
My favourite dessert in the world! A rich, white wine with sweetness and acidity is the right choice for this amazing dessert.

WHITE CHOCOLATE

White chocolate is not really a chocolate because it doesn't contain cocoa liquor. For more flavour, look for white chocolate that contains cocoa butter, not vegetable shortening. White chocolate consists of about 30 percent fat, 30 percent milk and about 30 percent sugar and vanilla. It has a shorter shelf life than dark chocolate because of the milk.

White Chocolate and Raspberry Tart

This is essentially a white chocolate truffle mixture studded with raspberries and encased in a pastry shell. It is a favourite on any dessert table.

PASTRY:
2 cups all-purpose flour
¾ cup butter, cubed
1 tbsp granulated sugar
1 egg, beaten
1 tbsp water

FILLING:
1 lb good-quality white chocolate, chopped
5 tbsp butter
⅔ cup whipping cream
2 cups fresh raspberries

Place flour, ¾ cup butter and sugar in food processor and pulse until fine crumbs form. Add egg and water. Pulse again until ball of dough forms.

Roll out dough and place in 11-inch flan pan. Chill for 15 to 20 minutes.

Preheat oven to 400°F.

Cover dough with sheet of foil and weight with dried beans or pastry weights. Bake for 20 minutes or until pastry is lightly browned. Remove foil and beans and bake for 5 to 8 minutes longer.

Melt chocolate and 5 tbsp butter in double boiler over hot (not boiling) water. Stir in cream; remove from heat and let cool slightly.

Arrange raspberries over bottom of pastry shell and cover with chocolate mixture. Refrigerate for at least 4 hours before serving.

Makes 10 to 12 servings.

ILLY ESPRESSO CANADA LTD. [SAL COSTANZA]

Order an espresso or cappuccino made with Illy coffee and you take perfection for granted. It's an assumption that is only possible because of the extraordinary effort the company makes to source and process the finest beans. The story of Illy begins in Trieste, Italy, in 1933, when Francesco Illy founded illycaffè and developed a method for storing and transporting coffee beans in pressurized metal containers. Suddenly the flavour and aroma of coffee could be preserved for years instead of days. Illy's descendants still run the firm, dedicated to educating their customers around the world in the exact science of making great espresso.

The Perfect Caffe Latte

The morning drink of Italy—strong coffee brewed in a stovetop coffee pot and combined with milk heated just to the boiling point. The ratio should be half and half, but some people prefer one part coffee to two or three parts milk.

For the bar version of caffe latte—the one we know in North America—a 1-oz "shot" of espresso is added to 5 to 7 oz steamed milk and topped with a dollop of foamed milk.

To make a perfect caffe latte, prewarm every part of the machine that will come in contact with the coffee, make sure any old coffee residue has been cleaned off, use only freshly ground, good-quality espresso, and tamp the espresso down firmly.

LOBLAWS

[TED READER]

RASPBERRY PUREE

Puree 2 cups frozen or fresh raspberries and add granulated sugar to taste. Stir in ¼ cup Framboise, then press sauce through sieve to remove the seeds.

In 1991, Second Harvest was a little-known entity to Loblaws Supermarkets and its employees. At that time, only one Loblaws Supermarket, City Farms, made occasional donations of bakery products to the food rescue program. But this has changed—in a very big way. In close cooperation with Loblaws management, the Second Harvest operations team established a program to roll out participation store by store, until all twenty-nine Toronto Loblaws stores were signed on to donate surplus food.

Loblaws now leads the way in supermarket food recovery as Second Harvest's largest donor of perishable food. A Second Harvest truck route is allocated exclusively, seven days a week, to collect donations from Loblaws Supermarkets. In the 1998–99 fiscal year, Loblaws donated 1,590,961 pounds of nutritious food—meat, deli products, produce and bakery products—to Second Harvest.

The vast increase in food donations has fostered two important benefits for Second Harvest and the agencies it serves. First, with more food to distribute, the organization is able to feed more people. Second, the agencies have gained access to an eclectic variety of fresh foods, which allows them to serve fresh and well-balanced meals.

The contribution of fresh foods by Loblaws Supermarkets makes a positive impact, every day, on the nutrition and quality of life of thousands of people in Toronto who rely on social agencies for hunger relief.

Ted Reader was the corporate chef at Loblaws when he created this recipe.

WINE SUGGESTIONS
Ontario Framboise 🍁
California Black Muscat dessert wine
Choose something sweet with a pronounced fruit flavour.

Peanut Butter and Jam Cheesecakes

peanut butter and jam

These cakes taste like peanut butter and jam sandwiches, but are much richer. Definitely for the kid in all of us. For a more grownup presentation, drizzle the cakes with raspberry puree (page 162).

---

12 peanut butter cookies
1 lb cream cheese, at room temperature
½ cup granulated sugar
2 eggs
2 tbsp lemon juice

1 tsp vanilla
2 tbsp raspberry jam
2 cups vanilla ice cream
12 sprigs fresh mint
Fresh raspberries

Preheat oven to 325°F.

Place cookies in bottom of 12 buttered and floured muffin cups, trimming cookies if necessary so they sit flat.

Beat cream cheese with sugar using electric beaters until light and fluffy. Add eggs one at a time, beating just until each one is incorporated. Blend in lemon juice and vanilla.

Spoon batter evenly over cookies, filling each muffin cup two-thirds full. Spoon ½ tsp raspberry jam into centre of each cake and swirl with toothpick.

Bake in centre of oven for 20 to 25 minutes or just until set. Cool in pan on rack for about 1 hour. Run small paring knife around edge of each cake to loosen. Unmould onto plate. Cover loosely with plastic wrap and refrigerate for at least 2 hours. Bring to room temperature before serving.

Place cheesecakes, cookie side down, on serving plates. Top each cake with small scoop of ice cream. Garnish with mint and raspberries.

Makes 12 servings.

ORO

[STEVE SONG]

CHOCOLATE STREUSEL

Sift 1¼ cups granulated sugar, 2 cups cocoa and 2 cups all-purpose flour into bowl. With hands, work 1¾ cups cold butter into flour mixture until large crumbs form. Chill for 30 minutes. Spread on rimmed baking sheet and bake in preheated 350°F oven for 15 minutes. Cool. Rub streusel through hands to break into smaller chunks.

"Even now, people are incredulous," muses Domenico Ciccocioppo. "They can hardly come to terms with the evolution!" It's true. The changes that he and his wife, Connie, made to their beloved restaurant were radical and brave, but they have brought golden dividends. Old Angelo's, founded in 1922, needed a makeover, but it received a whole new identity when it became Oro three years ago, with Chris Klugman and Dario Tomaselli leading the menu firmly towards the new millennium. Chris moved on, but Dario remains, with Oscar Turchi sharing the toque as chef de cuisine. "Dario's such a generous fellow," explains Domenico. "For the 1999 Taste he asked Steve to provide the recipe and receive the kudos." This is the recipe.

WINE SUGGESTIONS
Ontario Framboise or BC "port" ☙
Australian Liqueur Muscat
Only a fortified sweet wine could stand up to the mouth-coating character of milk chocolate.

Milk Chocolate Brûlée Tart with Lavender-infused Raspberry Compote

The silky, slightly runny custard and tart raspberries make this a pleasure for the palate. Sprinkle the tart with chocolate streusel if desired, for a fine finishing touch.

PASTRY:
½ cup butter, at room temperature
¼ cup granulated sugar
1 egg, beaten
1¼ cups cake and pastry flour

MILK CHOCOLATE BRÛLÉE:
1½ cups whipping cream
1 vanilla bean, split

¾ cup chopped milk chocolate
5 egg yolks
⅓ cup granulated sugar

RASPBERRY COMPOTE:
2 cups raspberries
1 cup granulated sugar
2 tbsp dried lavender
1 tbsp grated lemon rind

Beat butter in bowl until soft. Add ¼ cup sugar in thin, steady stream, beating until light and fluffy. Beat in half the egg until mixture is smooth. Beat in remaining egg until soft and fluffy.

Sift flour over butter mixture and mix until just combined. Press into disc and wrap in plastic. Refrigerate until firm, 2 to 4 hours.

Preheat oven to 425°F. Roll out pastry into circle on lightly floured surface. Fit into 9- or 10-inch tart pan with removable bottom. Trim edges. Refrigerate for 30 minutes. Prick bottom of pastry with fork and bake on centre rack of oven for about 15 minutes or until golden brown.

Combine cream and vanilla bean in saucepan and bring to boil; remove from heat. Stir in chocolate until blended.

Combine egg yolks with ⅓ cup sugar in bowl over barely simmering water. Whisk until thick, about 15 minutes. Pour reserved chocolate mixture into egg yolks, whisking constantly. Cook, stirring, for 15 to 20 minutes or until custard has thickened and coats back of spoon. Strain through fine sieve into bowl. Pour into baked tart shell. Refrigerate overnight.

Combine raspberries, 1 cup sugar, lavender and lemon rind in saucepan and cook over medium heat until sugar dissolves and raspberries are partially broken up, about 5 minutes. Remove from heat; chill.

Serve tart with raspberry compote and sprinkle with chocolate streusel (page 164) if desired.

Makes 8 servings.

PAULINE'S PASTRIES [ROBYN PERLMUTAR]

PIPING BAG

For a simple piping bag, cut the corner off a plastic bag.

Robyn Perlmutar's fabulous Chocolate Caramel Cloud was a great hit at Taste '98 and also won an award at the Canadian Fine Food Show. A tower of meringue, whipped cream and caramel, it's just one of the sophisticatedly scrumptious desserts, pastries and cheesecakes that her company, Pauline's Pastries, has given Toronto over the past twenty years—always made with the finest ingredients and always delivered fresh. You could say baking is a family trait where Robyn is concerned, and has been since the early 1900s, when her grandparents opened their bakery in Kensington Market.

WINE SUGGESTIONS
Canadian sweet "sherry"-style dessert wine ❧
Tawny Port
A sweet, fortified wine lightly chilled is a great match.

Chocolate Caramel Clouds

A crunchy base and soft billowy cream coated with caramel drizzle—this is pure heaven.

CHOCOLATE MERINGUES:
4 egg whites
1½ cups granulated sugar
3 tbsp cocoa
1 tbsp cornstarch

CARAMEL:
1 cup granulated sugar
½ cup water
½ cup whipping cream

WHIPPED CREAM:
1 cup whipping cream
¼ cup granulated sugar

Preheat oven to 250ºF. Line 2 large baking sheets with parchment paper. With pencil, draw eight 6-inch circles on paper. Turn parchment paper over on baking sheets.

Beat egg whites in large bowl until soft peaks form. Slowly add 1¼ cups sugar, ¼ cup at a time, making sure sugar is dissolved before next addition. Beat until stiff peaks form.

Sift together cocoa, cornstarch and remaining ¼ cup sugar. Fold into whites until well blended.

Spoon or pipe meringue mixture onto circles on baking sheets. Bake meringues for about 2 hours or until dry.

Cook 1 cup sugar with water in heavy saucepan over low heat, stirring until sugar dissolves. Increase heat to medium-high and boil until mixture turns amber, about 8 minutes. Brush down sides of pan with pastry brush dipped in water to avoid crystals. Remove from heat. Stir in whipping cream until combined and let cool. Reserve.

Beat whipping cream with ¼ cup sugar until stiff. Pipe or spoon whipped cream over meringues and drizzle with caramel.

Makes 8 servings.

RAHIER PATISSERIE [FRANÇOIS RAHIER]

Suddenly, in the summer of 1996, there was Rahier. Leaside gourmets queued at dawn outside the little store on Bayview Avenue where charming Sonia sold the exquisite mousses, perfect croissants and lemon-filled bichons, fruit tarts, cramique bread and spiced ginger cookies that her husband, François, baked every day. He had learned to make such immaculate confections from Belgium's top pâtissiers, and in no time at all Toronto was beating a path to his door. Eventually the crowds grew so large that the Rahiers expanded into the next-door premises; last year they took on partners, Marc and Sandra Tournayre, two restauranteurs from the Auvergne, "but we had become too used to doing things our own way," says Sonia, "so the partnership dissolved"—amicably, like everything else at Rahier.

WINE SUGGESTIONS
Canadian fortified wines—"sherry" or "port" style ❧
Cream Sherry or Bual Madeira
A sweet, fortified wine and these tuiles would make the perfect tea-time treat.

Coconut Tuiles

A lovely white cookie to serve with fruit, ice cream or to top a lemon dessert. They can be flat or molded.

¾ cup icing sugar
¾ cup shredded coconut
2 tbsp all-purpose flour

¼ cup whipping cream
2 egg whites
1 tbsp melted butter

Preheat oven to 350°F. Line baking sheets with parchment paper.

Combine icing sugar, coconut and flour in large bowl. Stir in cream and egg whites. Stir in melted butter.

Pipe or spoon tuile mixture onto baking sheets in 1 tbsp mounds. Flatten balls with fork dipped in water.

Bake for 8 minutes or until edges are dark brown. Remove to a rack to cool or slide off baking sheet while still hot and mould around a rolling pin or the handle of a wooden spoon. (They can also be quickly shaped by hand into cones and filled with ginger-flavoured whipped cream or white chocolate ganache.)

Makes 50 to 60 tuiles.

ROSEWATER SUPPER CLUB

[CHRISTOPHER KLUGMAN]

ITALIAN MERINGUE

In an Italian meringue, boiling sugar syrup is added to beaten egg whites. This makes the mixture stiff without adding gelatin. Buttercream icings are often made using this method.

Nick Di Donato's company, Liberty Entertainment, has a broad portfolio. Over the years he has created night clubs, sports bars, hip dance spots and restaurants large and small, but the emphasis has always been on entertainment—places that please all the senses, transcending genre. He opened Rosewater Supper Club, a sumptuously renovated neo-classical edifice on Toronto Street, in 1996, but hiring Chris Klugman as chef a year later added the finishing touch. A veteran of Scaramouche, Stadtländer's, Karin, Bistro 990, King Ranch and Oro, Klugman has always been marked by a rare intelligence and a light touch, but he can handle big numbers, too—a valuable asset now that he is corporate chef of Di Donato's empire.

WINE SUGGESTIONS
Canadian Icewine ✾
California Late Harvest Riesling or sweet Vouvray (Loire)
Lemon flavours need a white wine with sweetness as well as good acidity.

Lemon Brûlée Tartlets

lemon brûlée

These golden-topped little tarts are very delicate. Serve after a heavy meal and garnish with edible flowers and fresh blueberries, if desired.

¼ cup cornstarch	Finely grated rind and juice of 2 lemons
⅓ cup granulated sugar	¼ cup water
3 egg yolks	2 egg whites
1 cup milk	8 round shortbread cookies
¼ vanilla bean	¼ cup granulated sugar

Whisk together cornstarch, 2 tbsp sugar and egg yolks in bowl until pale in colour.

Heat milk, vanilla bean and lemon rind in saucepan on medium-high heat until small bubbles appear around edges and milk is steaming.

Add hot milk to egg mixture a bit at a time, whisking constantly. Return mixture to saucepan. Bring to boil over medium heat, stirring constantly. Cook for 3 minutes, stirring, until thickened and no longer starchy tasting. Remove from heat and stir in lemon juice. Strain through sieve.

Combine remaining ¼ cup sugar with water in very small saucepan. Bring to boil and cook until candy thermometer reads 240°F or drop of mixture forms hard ball when dropped into cold water.

Beat egg whites with electric mixer until stiff peaks form. Pour in boiling syrup in steady stream, beating constantly until cool, about 3 minutes.

Fold meringue into lemon mixture. Divide among 8 oiled non-stick custard cups or muffin cups. Top each cup with a shortbread cookie. Chill until firm, about 2 hours.

Unmould tartlets onto baking sheet. Sprinkle each with 1 tsp sugar. Place under preheated broiler, watching constantly, until sugar melts and turns golden, about 2 minutes.

Makes 8 servings.

SANCI TROPICAL FOODS [SAL BORG]

Now we know what was in the amazing Jamaican sangria Sal Borg served up at Taste '99! We also know where to get the ingredients: in Kensington Market on Kensington Avenue, where Sal's little emporium stands demurely behind its sidewalk displays of tart tamarillos, huge avocados, giant red papayas flown in from Trinidad, uglis and sapadilla. When he opened the store in 1914, Sal's grandfather sold only bananas—you can still see the hooks in the ceiling where he hung the great bunches. Bananas seemed deeply exotic in those days. Our knowledge has grown, but Sanci is still the place to discover ripe tropical fruit of the finest quality.

Jamaican Sangria

Every year at Toronto Taste Sal Borg makes this Jamaican Sangria which appears to be very mild until you feel the kick it delivers. This is a great punch for a summer party. Passion fruit concentrate and sorrel syrup can be purchased at any West Indian store; if unavailable, use passion fruit juice and orange juice.

2 750 mL bottles white rum
2 750 mL bottles dry red wine
1 750 mL bottle Jamaican sorrel syrup
2 cups passion fruit concentrate
8 cups sparkling water
4 cups orange juice

Juice of 4 limes
Juice of 4 lemons
Ice
4 oranges, sliced
4 lemons, sliced
4 limes, sliced

Place rum, wine, sorrel syrup, passion fruit concentrate, sparkling water, orange juice, lime juice and lemon juice in very large punch bowl. Mix in ice.

Garnish with sliced oranges, lemons and limes.

For a party of 20.

LISA SLATER

CARAMEL SAUCE

Combine 1 cup granulated sugar, ¼ cup water and 1 tbsp corn syrup in heavy saucepan. Bring to boil over high heat, reduce heat to medium and simmer until sugar caramelizes to a deep golden brown, about 5 minutes. (To avoid burning, remove saucepan from heat just before caramel becomes golden brown.) Stirring constantly, carefully pour in 1 cup whipping cream (it splatters). Cook until sauce is a pourable consistency, about 6 to 8 minutes.

Makes about 1½ cups.

Lisa Slater grew up in the food business in New York City, where she opened her first restaurant, Slotnick's Daughter. She came to Toronto in 1979 to run her family's coffee company, Goodhouse Foods, and stayed to create a string of successful enterprises with her sister Abigail: The Original Bakery Café, The Original Bakery in Forest Hill and on Yonge Street, Dakota Kitchens and BagelWorks. One of the co-chairs of the first ever Taste and a founder and co-chair of Eat to the Beat, the gala event at which the city's top women chefs raise funds to fight breast cancer, Lisa is also retail director of Sen5es Restaurant and Bakery.

This fabulous cake was always a runaway bestseller at The Original Bakery. The recipe is adapted from Rose Levy Beranbaum's *The Cake Bible*.

WINE SUGGESTIONS
Canadian sweet "sherry" 🍁
10- or 20-year-old Tawny Port
Chocolate is difficult to match with wine; best to choose fortified wine with some sweetness.

Banana Chocolate Chip Pecan Caramel Cake

If you like, you can omit the chocolate chips or pecans. This cake has lots of rich flavour without them.

---

1 cup mashed ripe bananas	½ cup + 2 tbsp butter, at room temperature
2 tbsp buttermilk	¾ cup + 2 tbsp granulated sugar
2 eggs	¾ cup chocolate chips
1 tsp vanilla	1 cup coarsely chopped toasted pecans
¾ cup all-purpose flour	½ cup whipping cream
1 cup cake and pastry flour	4 oz bittersweet chocolate, chopped
1 tsp baking soda	¾ cup caramel sauce (page 174)
1 tsp baking powder	¼ cup chopped toasted pecans
½ tsp salt	

Preheat oven to 350°F. Oil a 12-cup bundt pan. Stir together bananas, buttermilk, eggs and vanilla in bowl.

Sift together flours, baking soda, baking powder and salt in separate bowl.

Beat butter in electric mixer on medium speed until light and fluffy, about 2 minutes. Gradually add sugar, scraping down sides after 1 minute. Continue to beat for 2 minutes or until mixture is light and fluffy.

Beat in half the wet ingredients gradually. Beat in half the dry ingredients. Repeat with remaining wet and dry ingredients.

Scrape down sides of bowl and gently fold in chocolate chips and coarsely chopped pecans. Pour batter into bundt pan and smooth top.

Bake for 30 to 45 minutes or until top is deep golden brown and cake springs back when gently pressed or toothpick comes out with a moist crumb on it. Cool in pan on rack for about 30 minutes.

Place whipping cream in small saucepan and bring to boil. Remove from heat and whisk in chopped chocolate. Cool.

Unmould cake on rack set over baking sheet. Cool completely. Pour chocolate glaze over top of cake, allowing it to roll down sides. Allow to cool.

Drizzle ½ to ¾ cup caramel sauce over cake and sprinkle evenly with chopped pecans.

Makes 12 servings.

WANDA'S PIE IN THE SKY [WANDA BEAVER]

FRUIT PIES

Always bake fruit pies on the lower shelf of the oven to help the base brown. Bake for 15 minutes at a high heat to set the pastry, then reduce the heat to finish baking. This results in a firm pastry and tender filling.

Wanda Beaver created her company fifteen years ago while she was still a hard-working student at the Ontario College of Art. In those days she took the subway to deliver her pies by hand; now the business has grown into a full-scale wholesale operation supplying a range of sweets to restaurants and cafés across Toronto. She has also opened two retail locations so that more people than ever can bite into her famously flaky pastry crusts and tangy fruit fillings. Wanda describes her recipe for Taste '94, Wanda's Wonderful Peach Melba Pie, as "a celebration of the fruits of Canada. Niagara peaches are among the best in the world, juicy and flavourful, and B.C. raspberries are so large and yet so tender." With her background, it's no wonder Wanda's pies are works of art.

WINE SUGGESTIONS
Canadian Icewine or Select Late Harvest Vidal ❦
German Riesling Auslese
or California Late Harvest Sauvignon Blanc
The peachy character of Late Harvest wines make an ideal companion
for this delicious pie.

Wonderful Peach Melba Pie

This summer fruit pie is as good to look at as it is to eat.

PASTRY:
2¼ cup all-purpose flour
¼ tsp salt
1 cup shortening
⅓ cup ice water

FILLING:
1½ lb peaches, peeled and sliced
¾ cup granulated sugar

¼ cup cornstarch
½ tsp grated orange rind
2 cups fresh raspberries

TOPPING:
¾ cup slivered almonds
½ cup granulated sugar
½ cup all-purpose flour
¼ cup butter, cold

Stir together 2¼ cups flour and salt in large bowl. In food processor or with pastry blender, cut in shortening until crumbly. Add ice water and gently mix together with fork just until ball forms. Remove one-third of dough and shape into ball. Shape remaining two-thirds of dough into second ball. Wrap with plastic wrap and refrigerate for 30 minutes.

Preheat oven to 425°F. Roll larger piece of dough on lightly floured surface into circle about ⅛ inch thick. Fit into 11-inch flan pan, trimming and folding under excess around the edge.

Combine peaches, ¾ cup sugar, cornstarch and orange rind in bowl.

Spread raspberries in single layer over bottom crust. Spread peach mixture on top.

Roll out remaining pastry and cut into strips ¾ inch wide. Weave a loose lattice on top of fruit. Pinch edges to seal with crust.

Combine almonds, ½ cup sugar, ½ cup flour and butter in food processor or with pastry blender until crumbly. Sprinkle crumble over pie.

Place pan on baking sheet and bake for 15 minutes. Reduce heat to 350°F and bake for 45 to 60 minutes or until pastry is golden brown and fruit is bubbling.

Makes 10 to 12 servings.

WINSTON'S

[MICHAEL POTTERS]

How sumptuous Winston's table looked at Taste '98, draped with richly coloured fabrics and shadowed by towering floral displays! And there was chef Michael Potters, surrounded by the glamour, flambéing morels in green Chartreuse and stuffing them into miniature vol-au-vent cases. Meanwhile the crowds emptied his trays of foie gras, lemon smoked salmon and chocolate Kahlua opera cake, the recipe Potters shares with us now. The elaborate classical menu typified the style of the newly reincarnated Winston's—opulent, expensive and, like some exotic bloom, sadly short-lived. For Potters, given carte blanche in the kitchen, it was a chance to cook with the sort of ingredients few kitchens can afford, a fascinating interlude in a career that has led him from Ivory to Left Bank and Rosewater Supper Club, and now to Accolade.

WINE SUGGESTIONS
Canadian "port"-style fortified wine ❦
Ruby Port
A rich dessert like this deserves a sweet fortified wine to set off the chocolate flavour.

Chocolate Kahlua Opera Cake

This rich, imposing layer cake has many parts and it takes time to put it together, but the final result will exceed your expectations. It is a beautiful classic French cake that would also make a simple and elegant wedding cake.

ALMOND SPONGE:
5 eggs
½ cup granulated sugar
1 cup ground almonds
½ cup cake and pastry flour
6 egg whites
Pinch salt
2 tbsp icing sugar

BUTTERCREAM:
¼ cup granulated sugar
2 tbsp water
2 egg yolks
1 egg

2 tsp vanilla
1 cup butter, at room temperature

CHOCOLATE GANACHE:
1 cup whipping cream
¼ cup corn syrup
1 lb bittersweet chocolate, chopped
2 tbsp butter

KAHLUA SYRUP:
1 cup double-strength coffee
¼ cup Kahlua

¼ cup cocoa

Preheat oven to 400°F. Line 17½ x 11½-inch jellyroll pan with parchment paper.

Beat 5 eggs and ½ cup sugar in large bowl with electric mixer until thick and pale yellow. Sift almonds and flour into egg mixture and fold in.

Beat egg whites with salt in separate bowl until soft peaks form (use clean beaters). Gradually beat in icing sugar until mixture forms stiff peaks. Fold into almond-flour mixture.

Spread batter smoothly over prepared pan. Bake for about 20 minutes or until golden brown. Cool in pan on rack.

Combine ¼ cup sugar and water in saucepan over medium heat and cook until sugar dissolves and reaches soft ball stage (240°F on candy thermometer).

Beat egg yolks with 1 egg and vanilla in bowl with electric mixer until thick and pale yellow. Slowly pour sugar syrup into eggs while continuing to beat on low speed. Beat until cool.

Cut 1 cup butter into cubes and beat into egg-syrup mixture one cube at a time until smooth. Refrigerate.

Heat whipping cream and corn syrup to boil in saucepan. Pour over chocolate and stir in 2 tbsp butter. Stir until melted and smooth.

Combine coffee and Kahlua in small bowl.

Cut sponge into 4 equal rectangles. Brush one layer with Kahlua syrup and sift 1 tbsp cocoa over top. Spread with ¾ cup buttercream. Top with second layer of cake. Brush with Kahlua syrup and sift cocoa over; spread with 1¼ cups ganache. Repeat third layer with ¾ cup buttercream and fourth layer with 1¼ cups ganache to cover top. Let filling drip down sides of cake. Refrigerate.

Trim sides and cut cake into small squares.

Makes 8 to 12 servings.

INDEX

LUCY WAVERMAN is the author of such national best-selling cookbooks as *Dinner Tonight* and *Fast and Fresh*. She writes a weekly national food column for the *Globe and Mail* and also appears regularly on Citytv's "Cityline." Waverman is the food consultant for the LCBO and food editor of its publication, *Food & Drink*.

JAMES CHATTO is the food and restaurant columnist of *Toronto Life* magazine, senior editor of *Food & Drink* and food editor of *Gardening Life* magazine. His third book, *The Man Who Ate Toronto: Memoirs of a Restaurant Lover*, has just been reissued in paperback.

TONY ASPLER is the most widely read wine writer in Canada. He is the wine columnist for the *Toronto Star*, editor of *Winetidings* magazine and the author of many books on wine and food including *The Wine Lover's Companion*, the recently reissued *Vintage Canada* and *The Wine Lover Cooks* (co-authored with Kathleen Sloan).